# *I'll Die Dancing*

*by Fay Siravo*

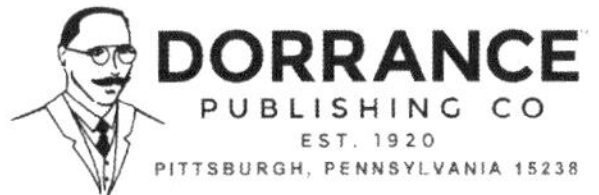

Dorrance Publishing Co
585 Alpha Drive
Pittsburgh, PA 15238
Visit our website at *www.dorrancebookstore.com*

ISBN: 978-1-4809-3900-4
eISBN: 978-1-4809-3877-9

Doctors have always said, and I truly believe, a child never remembers anything before the age of five-years-old. This is also proven to be true with adult diabetes that strikes exactly at the age of forty. This happened to my husband for which we were married forty-three years, and it would have been forty-four, had he lived on November 7, 2014. We got married, if it were a Tuesday on an Election Day– if you were voting for a mayor, governor, vice president, president, judge, etc. – only it was a Saturday on November 7, 1970, as my husband and I are Roman Catholic. I will get back to my adult years later in my story. I will bring you to my remembrance at the age of five-years-old.

I was holding my hand with my grandfather. His name in the United States was Charles Embris. He was Lithuanian and from Lithuania. I was half Lithuanian because of my grandfather and half Irish, from my father, whom I never seen alive. My grandpop brought me to a place that I did not know, and there was a woman in a small cell that looked like a jail with bars. My grandfather, who was her father but I did not know who she was at the time, was coming to visit her and brought me. When we got close to the cell, she seen him and violently started grasping at the bars and yelling to him, "Get me out of here, get me out of here." I was extremely scared and held on to my grandpop's trouser leg. There were three nice black nurses that led her away from my grandfather as she was mad when she saw him and really did not notice me with him. I was her real daughter which I did not know until later. Her name was Anne. The place and cell was Byberry State Hospital.

Time passed and my mother, Anne, came home. She was absolutely beautiful. She was quiet, had dark black brown hair (natural) at the time. She was around forty- or forty-one-years-old. As I was born exactly in 1950, I had seen her for the first time at five-years-old, and later she told me that she was thirty-six-years-old when she had me. My mom and I went to a Catholic church every Sunday for Sunday mass, which was named "Saint George's," a Roman Catholic Lithuanian church. The church was a small church, and there were a lot of stairs to climb before you even got into the church, a typical old church. It wasn't a fancy or really beautiful church like a lot of the other old churches, but it was our church, of our descent. We had strict nuns and priests who always wore their habits, nuns' gowns and priests' gowns with their Christ cross necklaces. They were black for every day unless for masses which were other colors. They (the nuns) were never allowed to take their habits off, which were coverings to not show their hair, only when they would go to sleep in their rooms. It was very strict in those days, in my early years of the 1950s.

My mom was very close to the nuns. It was time now for my mom to enter me into school as I was still five-years-old. I can remember her wanting me to go to school at St. George's, as there also was a Catholic school in addition to the church and the convent all connected together and close on the same grounds. My mother at the time after she was a famous movie star, became a waitress for a famous restaurant food chain named Horn and Hardart's. She also worked for PTC, which means Pennsylvania Transportation Corporation, and today is named SEPTA, which is Southeastern Pennsylvania Transportation Association. I don't have any idea why they changed the name or style, especially the women, they dressed so high class. They wore olive green short jackets, long straight mid-calf skirts with a kick pleat in the back, and in winter, they wore matching slacks, which are pants if you don't know. The men wore the same with jackets and pants. I think they may have been called CPO jackets, which meant Chief Petty Officer.

To get back to my mother having to make a decision for me to go to school, she was talking it over with the nuns, and I remember she was afraid because she worked and I would have to walk alone as it was two long blocks and my grandpop was getting old. There was a public school named James Martin only one block from my house which my mom felt it would be better as another friend of hers had a little boy, and she offered to my mom to take me to school with him. I was happy to go to school at James Martin in Port Richmond, a section in Philadelphia located at Richmond and Ontario streets. I lived at 2718 E. Madison St., a small house in the middle of the street and a very famous house when I was growing up as my grandfather (Charles Embris) built a big three-story hall, nightclub, and supper club right around the corner of our house, which still stands today, with other Lithuanian men. It was called The Big Lit, for modern terms as I had a real smart first uncle named Frank and nicknamed Frankie, and he was tough and unique and dressed very well. My grandmother, whose namc was Albena, came here with my grandfather with their four children from Lithuania. My mom, Anne, was the first born; then her brother, Frank; then her brother, John, who looked identical to the famous (known for cowboy movies) John Wayne and had the same persona, and he was tough; then there was the last of the four siblings named Carol.

The Lithuanian music hall, nicknamed The Big Lit, was huge. Famous singing groups sang there such as The Ink Spots with Gene Chandler, known for the famous song "Duke of Earl." I don't remember any other groups singing there, only them, as I was too young and going to school. A lot of them have passed for which they could have told me a lot, as I believe you learn from the grandads and moms who were in the tough business of music.

I love music, and to me, it is one of the greatest gifts in the world. The one thing I don't like is music that is pushed on you that you don't like, such as hard rock and music in the same category that gets very insane and you can't enjoy it, or even dance to it, if you call that dancing and music what you still call today in the year 2014. What you or I thought was corny in music and dancing in reality is not corny, such as the dancers and singers of the Lawrence Welk Show. You try to do that and see how hard it is. It takes years to learn and practice. Even the famous Lady Gaga has changed and captures her excellence in music with a concert doing a duet with the famous Tony Bennett, who has never lost his famous voice, class, or style. The famous Madonna, for which she originally started as a dancer and said she would never be singer, pursued her career and shined in the first Vogue tour concert, bringing back the great Hollywood past with her excellent video, "Living in a Material World," reminiscent of the famous Marilyn Monroe. Everyone naturally knows there was only one Marilyn Monroe and Norma Jean, but it's great to see these new stars that have so much talent simulate them.

Someone once said, and I don't know who it was but it's a great quote, "In order to see the present, you had to see the past." We learn from the past, and change isn't always progress. I sure do miss my old Black Bell telephone from the famous Alexander Graham Bell, a corded phone and my mom put locks on it when I was a teenager, because it was expensive even then for frivolous talk.

Well, I am going to bring you back to my childhood. I started kindergarten at the age of six. We had a beautiful teacher named Mrs. Smith. Every day before going to our classrooms, we would go to auditorium first. The principal would speak, and even though it was a public school, we said the Lord's Prayer every day. We had art classes always in kindergarten, and Mrs. Smith read us stories. We were good children, and we would have rest periods and naps on cots in a separate room to freshen before going back to class. It was a half-hour day in the afternoon about three or four hours, and we were home by 3 or 3:30 PM. As time went on in kindergarten, we went to school in the morning hours instead of afternoon as the school board was preparing us for the future workforce and the basic morning work of 9 AM to 5 PM after we graduated high school. I went to kindergarten in the morning hours, and it was told to us that after school there is recreation at the school at about 4 or 5 or 6 PM, and we were home before dark.

I think that I made a mistake and am now remembering that I went to kindergarten first for half of the year in the afternoon, then the second half year in the morning. I would come home to my grandpop and tell him I have to go back to school, which was called After School Recreation, and I was happy to want to go and not be hungry. There was another teacher, I don't know her name but she said that you could pick any room you wanted to go to. I went into one room, and there were little houses you could play with, plaster of Paris milk bottles, blocks, and other learning toys. I left that room and went into another room, and for the first time, I heard music which attracted me to go into the room, having heard it from the hallway corridors.

There was a dance teacher teaching little girls, like me, something I never seen or knew about and later learned was tap dancing. The song she was playing on an old fashioned Victrola record machine was, which I later learned, "Tweedle Dee." It was such a happy song, and I came in wanting to join this class. The teacher was beautiful, and her name was Karen, which we became very close as I grew up. I loved learning to tap dance and would go every day after school. We had to get and buy a black and white marble hardback book. In those days, in the 1950s, they were only twenty-five cents. Karen taught us tap dancing steps daily, and we would write down the steps that we learned to practice at home. I had to be seven-years-old now and in the first grade because I learned to read and write.

Karen told us we had to get tap dancing shoes. I went home and told my mom. Every Saturday we would go shopping either in my neighborhood (Port Richmond), or in Kensington, which is next to Port Richmond in Philadelphia. There was the famous Baum's on Richmond St., that still stands today at the vicinity of 11th and Chestnut Street, for which I shopped in my growing teenage years alone. My mom brought me to the store, and the Baum's shoe salesman sized me with my tap dancing shoes. They were patent leather, and you got steel cleats with them, but you needed the old fashioned shoe repair men to put these on your tap dancing shoes. My mom and I brought them home, and diagonally across our street on Madison St., we had a shoemaker and shoe repair man. They were a married couple who had their own business and lived there. I put my tap dancing shoes with the shoe makers to have my cleats put on. We would get a ticket, and it would be written on the ticket and they would also tell us when the shoes would be done, usually within three to five days or one whole week.

I continued going to first grade every day, and tap dancing classes every day after school. We always were given homework assignments on weekdays, Monday through Friday. I would do my homework, and we were lucky that we had a new invention called the television, nicknamed TV, with a beautiful pale beige and darker brown like line designs through it, with four brown legs, and a twenty-five inch glass screen–typical of the TVs you see in the old black and white 1950s moves. I would look at the TV, and in my later teen years of about thirteen-years-old (which is adolescent teen years) and wonder, "where does that come from?" It really was a wonder.

There was a famous TV show named "The Sally Starr Show." I watched it every day when I went to kindergarten in my afternoon kindergarten years. "The Sally Starr Show" was on in the early morning hours of about 8 AM Eastern time here in Philadelphia, PA. Sally Starr was a beautiful cowgirl with natural platinum white hair and had beautiful cowgirl costumes. She was a Children's Hour TV show, and you learned a lot like that of the famous Sesame

Street you still see today. It was on channel twelve here in Philadelphia, Sesame Street that is, a Public Learning Station. "Sally Starr" was on channel six. We only had channels three, six, ten, and twelve here in Philadelphia, and we didn't have to pay for TV like you do today. Pay TV started here, if I can remember, in Philadelphia maybe in the mid-80s or early 90s. There were other children's morning TV shows and they were great, such as "The Gene London Show," "The Bernie Weber Show," "The Pete Boyle Show," and "The Chief Halftown Show." These shows were on Saturdays in the morning and the other famous TV show, "The Mickey Mouse Club." If only kids today had these TV shows. They would love it.

If only we could bring that good past back to this future to hand down. But too many passed away, and this generation may not have the skill to do that, or the knowledge. It's a shame for all generations to come, and for us. It has gotten out of hand, and I believe that it was the McCarthy Era when TV was censored. It was better, because TV was a luxury not to be taken for granted. They had no morals. They were jealous and wanted to have what you had and they were only what you would call "wannabes."

Like the immoral TV show you see today, "Family Feud," the immoral questions that black host asks. It was never that way when it was the original host. And it is disgusting and something should be done about it.

Well to get back to my childhood years, I forgot to mention something immoral that happened to me. The woman who used to walk me to school every day could not do it anymore. I think my mom was working as a waitress then, but I'm not sure. There was a family that moved in on the corner of Madison and Emery streets, right down the street from our house, which was between Salmon and Tilton streets. We were on Madison Street, on the corner of Salmon and Madison streets, and there was a grocery store. My family bought there always. My mom met a woman that was strange looking, not beautiful at all, fat, and dressed like a gypsy, but she was very nice. They had become friends, and my mom asked her if she could watch me after school, as I became friends with her little girl.

I first met her little girl in the summer of 1955 or 1956 as there was a steel pole on the corner of their house, which was a vehicle sign, and I was dressed up in a medium colored turquoise nylon eyelet dress with a crinoline slip and swinging my arm around the pole. A little girl came out, and we became friendly.

I brought her to our house to meet my mom and grandpa. That is how my mom and her mom initially became friends. So my mom felt comfortable as after school I would go to my friend's house until my mom would come for me after work, then we would go home right down the street. My mom always paid my friend's mom for watching me. My girlfriend's name was Vivian, and her mom's name was Marian. I felt very happy and comfortable, and Vivian was like a sister and my first girlfriend. She was a year younger than me, born April 14, 1951. She had a dad, and his name was Antonio. Marian, his wife, would call him Tony.

Practically every day after school, Vivian and I would be together as time went on, especially on weekends. I would want her to sleep at my house, and she would ask her dad if I could sleep over her house. Her dad was a good dad and strict. Vivian wanted me to sleep over her house for the first time, but her father was not in favor of this. So Vivian was allowed to stay at my house. It was summertime, and we were outside playing. I wanted to go in to get a toy, and when I came out I locked the door, because Vivian wanted me to sleep at her house. When we went to her house, she told her dad I locked the door and could not get back in because my mom and grandpop were sleeping, so her dad said that it was okay. We were so happy, because we took turns sleeping over each other's house in the summer when we had summer vacation from school.

Vivian's house was diagonally across from the famous Goodyear Tire Factory. Next to the Goodyear Tire Factory was, and still stands today, the trolley and bus loop. The number seventy-three bus runs, and I'm sure the number fifteen trolley runs. It is a beginning and end stop. You could see the bus number seventy-three from Vivian's house at Madison and Emery streets. To get the transportation now named SEPTA, you get on one block, and a short block, at Emery and Westmoreland streets, or on Richmond and Westmoreland streets, which shows on the number seventy-three on the SEPTA buses today, and there is a cyclone see-through fence in the same traditional way it was when I grew up in my childhood years of the 1950s. Thank God we still have that tradition to tell the new generation and remember our happy times. It's been a long time from the 1950s to now in the year 2014, and we were happy.

Vivian's house inside was old fashioned but not really beautiful like our house. We had a piano in the dining room as my uncle Frankie played the piano, and he had what you would call a great ear for music. We had piano rolls, for which you put in these piano rolls that looked like wallpaper rolls, and these rolls were perforated. You could put them in the piano, and the piano rolls like a curtain rod and push something. The piano played by itself. It was versatile, so if my uncle Frankie or any other family that didn't want to play the piano, the self-playing piano was great for family and friends parties.

Our house was finely furnished downstairs with dark brown dining room furniture, a dining room table, a buffet, dining room closet, and the piano. I don't know how my family ever fit that all in and it was perfect. Later in life, I hated dark brown furniture or any kind of dark furniture. The parlor was, I would say, considered modern 50s style. The sofa and chairs were evergreen. I can't remember anything more in the parlor except the sofa, chairs, and light beige TV. Our kitchen had wood cabinets painted a lighter green with white. We had a marble sink with normal old fashioned spigots, hot water on the left hand side and cold on the right hand side, and a stationary spout. Everything fit perfectly, not like all of the errors that are done today by faulty workmanship. But there is an old saying that holds true today: "You learn by your mistakes." Too many people are overworked and not paid enough, and the work they do as another old saying goes: "I could not pay you enough." There's too much greed and jealousy, and too many changes.

Change is not progress, especially in this too modern world. It's robbery. Everything is to make more money. Either way you fail, man has failed. We learn from our forefathers, and we miss them, the good ones that is, that suffered and passed, to make it better, and were highly skilled.

To get back on the subject of Vivian, my first girlfriend. She had what seemed a good family. She had three brothers for which in later years she told me that her two older brothers were from a different father. The oldest was named Eric. The next brother was named Brian, and her youngest brother, Joseph, was nicknamed Don. As time went on, Vivian and I stayed together in her house. We were still little, and I was in kindergarten. Her second half-brother, Brian, was sixteen-years-old. At night I would stay for dinner until my mom came, or when I stayed overnight as Vivian and I became, as I said before, very close. Sonya cooked great dinners, and it was my first time to eat spaghetti and meatballs. Later on Vivian told me as years passed, her father was Italian and her mother was Lebanese. That is when I was about thirteen-years-old that she told me, because she and I were too little to know about nationalities. Sonya also made cauliflower for dinner, for which they called Popeye, like the famous Popeye cartoons. It was the second yellow vegetable I ever ate as we ate only what I could remember as white potatoes.

Sonya was always jovial and strict with her sons as they were typical bad boys. They would clown around when their father was not there. Tony worked for PTC, now named SEPTA. There was a Sid's Market for which Sonya used to also buy her food, as my family on Richmond St., a couple of blocks past Allegheny Ave. One day, I think it was in May or June before summer vacation from school, it was a weekday and it was warm. I came home from school and went to Vivian's as usual before my mom came home. Sonya and Tony were not there. Only Vivian, her brothers (Brian and Joey), and I were there. It may have been a Saturday for which I stayed overnight from Friday. I was five- to six-years-old and in kindergarten. All I remember is having my below-the-knee accordion pleated skirt and blouse with knee socks, as my mom gave this to me for a Christmas present in a famous Lit Brothers box, which was located around 9th and Market streets, where the now famous Ross Store is located. The Lit Brothers box was a standard logo in light gold and white print and looked like a Philadelphia city print with horses and carriages and our famous Philadelphia city hall London-like clock, with trees. Lit Brothers had much more space than the Ross store for shopping and after the famous Lit Brothers store closed they used it for a temporary comedy club for upcoming famous comedians. Then it became the Ross store. Lit Brothers, the famous Gimbels store and famous Snellenburg department store were all connected before the gallery stores on Market St. Today it is not pleasurable to go shopping as there is a lot of misdirection. Sales people are unskilled, pushy, greedy, and degrade poor people, especially at Christmas time. Most of the owners are Jewish and just looking to make money. The unbelievable part is they don't even believe in Christ when Christmas is for those who believe in Christ–Jesus Christ that is, who died on a cross and it was Jews that killed Him. Before Christ there was nothing. He is my Lord and my God.

One time when I was hired as an independent worker for the perfume industry, which means you do not get paid from the stores where you sell the perfume, you get paid from the perfume companies. It was Strawbridge and Clothier at Neshaminy Mall in Neshaminy, PA. I was, for the first time, promoting a beautiful perfume for women called Halston. A woman came to the counter as I was working outside of the counter and I asked her, "Would you like to try some Halston? Turn your wrist and I'll spray it on your wrist." She like the fragrance and wanted to purchase it. She was a very nice, plain woman. I told her of the gift set that was priced for thirty-five dollars, and you get an extra free gift from Halston. The poor woman only had thirty-two. I said, "Stay here, and I'll talk to the manager," who was Linda. I asked Irene if the woman could have this and would the store be able to cover the three dollars. Irene said, "No." I really felt bad as I didn't have the money to cover it and told the lady. I wonder if the Strawbridge family, after having met this nice woman, would have done that. I doubt it, they would have given it to this lady.

After that first experience of that incident, I started watching all of these sales ladies and so-called managers. I saw them stealing from the perfume companies, carrying shopping bags of perfume for themselves. That was one bad incident. There was a lot of jealousy as I was considered a "fragrance model," and it was like a competition of who could sell the most, whether it be the fragrance models or salespeople of Strawbridge. There also was something else I learned as time went on. It was called "double dipping," which was cheating when you work for one perfume company who was paying you, and you were selling another fragrance and getting paid for both when you did not do the work for the other perfume company who was paying you. I discovered this when my boss from the perfume companies promoted me to be a coordinator, and I had to make schedules and help to hire models. I caught one girl double dipping at John Wanamaker's. That was my favorite, most beautiful department store. It was so expensive and elegant, the price tags even scared me to death. I was very grateful for having had the experience as a fragrance model, but it was not an easy job, although it's a glamorous one. I was so upset when John Wanamaker's was sold to Macy's.

But there's a reason for everything, and it's not my say, but the next upcoming generation will be missing a lot not knowing about John Wanamaker, especially at Christmas time, which is now Macy's. The inside Christmas light show is spectacular and dates back from when I was a child.

Going back to my childhood of around six, my grandma passed away. She was sixty-three-years-old. My grandpop was mean to her when he got drunk as he always went to the Lit Club that he built. Most of those men drank very heavily and got mean when they were drunk. I was so afraid that I'd say to my grandma when he came home, "Let's go hide in the cellar, Grandmom." One day he was out of his temper when she was sixty-two, which I believe contributed to her death. We were going down to the cellar, and he pushed her down the steps and she broke her arm. She died shortly after that and my grandpop raised me. I was always with Vivian most of the time, but her second brother, Brian, did a terrible thing to me that is too sinful to discuss when I was six-years-old.

There was a Lithuanian family down the street for which I became close to, a Patty Freeme, and they watched out for me. They did not like this Lebanese family who were half Italian because of their father Tony. They found out the strange and sinful things that the three brothers–, Eric, Brian and Don–were doing and wanted them prosecuted. I was in the house at Vivian's one summer night when the Freeme family told them to come out of their house. Tony went to the door and Sonya followed him outside. Tony was arguing with them and Sonya said, "Tony, don't," and she passed out on the sidewalk in front of their house. I quickly went home.

A couple of days passed and Vivian came over to my house and was crying bitterly. My mom was there, and Vivian told us her mother had a heart attack from the incident and died. We comforted Vivian, and she stayed with us for a couple of weeks. We didn't know her father was making plans to move, and he took Don and her to Southwest Philadelphia, where his family lived. As I got older, around thirteen, I would visit Vivian and vice versa. I stayed overnight, and Vivian seemed happier, although her father used to beat her. She may have done wrong things that I didn't see.

Later as years went on after I got married, Vivian got married to an Italian man and had three girls: Lois, Joyce, and Janice. I became godmother to Joyce. We did not see each other for years and lost touch for which in a way I was glad for that dark shadow of her brothers that hung over me. Eric, the oldest, was gay for which I did not know when I was little. I had a daughter who became an occupational therapist, graduating from Thomas Jefferson University, for which I told her to go into the medical field. About 2010, I got a phone call and there was a young, excited, happy woman who said, "Hi, this is Lois." I didn't know who it was, and she told me she worked with my daughter and that and their mothers grew up together for which it was Vivian's first daughter,

Lois. I was happy to hear from her, and she was calling to see and invite me to her mom's surprise birthday party. I told her that I would see because it was a long trip to where she lived and my husband had diabetes. We chatted and she said that her Uncle Brian was out in Texas, and she seemed happy and unknowing of what he did to me as it was kept hidden. I naturally was not happy because if we did make the surprise birthday party for Vivian he might have been there. We hung up and I sent and wrote Vivian a birthday card. It's too far for a one day party. Some people, most people,were not seeing how hard it was for their pleasure. When you want to have a party like this from those far away, you provide and pay for the transportation and have lodging. That's what you call a party!

To bring you back to my childhood days again, I was about seven-years-old in first grade, then went to second grade. I think that I may have been eight-years-old. There was a very nice black family. Their last name was Downs. They had a son by the name of Timothy, and he had brothers. Timothy's parents wanted him to go to a good school. I think that they may have originally come from the state of Washington, but I'm not absolutely sure. There were better white schools here so the Downs family resided here in Port Richmond in Philadelphia. They were the only black family and lived at the vicinity of Richmond and Venango streets, close to James Martin Elementary School like my house, only in opposite directions as I lived at the Richmond and Allegheny avenues section.

Timmy was a bad boy. In school, he did bach unspeakable things to me and did not have any interest in learning the right way for which his parents hoped for. We always were together in school. We had, in the month of May, a celebration called Maypole Day, and we learned how to do folk dancing to the song of "Little Brown Jug." I was paired with Timmy for this as I had pure snow-white hair. Timmy's family came for the celebration along with my grandpop. I can remember in my later adult years, the famous football player, Bubba Smith, being there. They all laughed at Timmy and I as we looked so cute together, doing folk dancing, even my grandpop. Bubba Smith may have been a relation to the Downs family. Time again passed, and I never said anything as I was only a child.

We had another recreation center at the playground at Richmond and Allegheny outside. I learned how to play Ball and Jacks and was pretty good at this game. I loved it. The athletic department said that there would be a Jacks and Ball contest coming up, and those who knew how to play can enter. I would then practice every day. I played with my two best new girlfriends which I didn't mention yet. They were identical twins, Erica and Joyce. I also played with my dance teacher, Karen. The Ball and Jacks contest was on a Sunday in the summer of July when we were on summer vacation from school at James Martin. I remember waking up that Sunday. My mom I slept in a pretty big front bedroom, and she was still sleeping. I was so excited, because this was the day to enter the contest, and I dashed to want to tell my grandpop who slept in a smaller backroom. When I went into his room, I was ready to say, "Grandpop I'm going to be in a Jacks contest today," but I found my poor grandpop lying on a full blooded mattress, and he was bleeding to death. I fell to my knees and said sadly, "Oh, Grandpop!" I ran to my mom's room and screamed, "Mom! Grandpop's bleeding." It was horrible with a full blooded mattress. I showed her, and she kept her calm as I stayed by my grandpop's bedside. My mom went downstairs to call the police on our black dial Bell telephone. Then, here in Philadelphia, the police number was 511, and the patrol wagons were red in color. Today the police cars and patrol wagons here in Philadelphia are white with decorative blue ribbons, and the police number is 911. Then it was the 1950s for me, and the police colors and phone number changed after the 1960s.

My mom quickly got a towel and woke my grandpop. The blood was coming from his left upper arm muscle. My mom and I saw that his whole muscle was cut out, and his skin was hanging down–that's why the mattress was totally saturated completely with blood. He was bleeding to death. Later on, we found out that someone had taken a knife and cut his muscle out to rob him. Unluckily, he only had ten cents in his black purse, and the robbers weren't successful. My grandpop walked home from his club by himself and could not talk, and I found him. The police came, I stayed home with my mom, and grandpop went to, I think, Northeastern Hospital, which was located around Cedar St. and Allegheny Ave. They grafted his skin from his thigh to mend the upper left arm where the muscle was cut out. Later on, we found out when Terrance Brown made a lot of white friends. It was him, Terrance Brown, and two other of my boy classmates, Bucky Kendorski and Rodney Cleaver, and I don't know who else. It was initiated from Terrance Brown, and they were only around my age then, of eight-years-old.

My grandpop lived, and we were very happy. After that incident, I did not go to school for a lot of weeks. A black female social worker, who was trying to hide and conceal the horrific incident of what happened to my grandfather, was from the school board and came to our house. She knocked on the door. I opened it and let her in. She wanted to take me away from my grandpop, and I said that my grandpop took care of me very well and that we were happy. The social worker left, and I continued to live my life with my grandfather, mother, and my Uncle Frankie.

When I was born it was hard times for my mom, my grandfather, and Uncle Frankie. They had faced World War II (which is world war number two) and the horrible Depression Era. I never seen my real father whose name was John Alex Wills. My family told me that he was a lieutenant for the army. The war broke out, and it was over. My Godfather, who is my real uncle named John, wanted to put me up for adoption when I was born because of all the tragedy of the war and Depression Era left from World War I and World War II. My father was not returning because he was inducted and drafted into the service which means he had no choice. He had to do this civic duty for the United States. Today, in our more modern times, you can just join, like a club.

For this reason my grandfather, my Uncle John, wanted to put me up for adoption. My Uncle Frankie, my favorite uncle who was like a father to me, would not allow my Uncle John to do this and said, "Nobody's gonna put our baby up for adoption." That is how my Uncle Frankie, Grandpop, and mom raised me. Later on, my Uncle John and his wife, Nellie, became my Catholic godparents, and my Uncle John was also a father to me and very protective of me. My Uncle John, who was a Marine and designed airplanes for the famous Boeing and Boeing aircraft corporation, set up airplane plants throughout the United States. He was highly intelligent, and my grandpop favored him because he went to college for and to study aeronautics. We even had our own private airplanes, because of my Uncle Johnny and Uncle Frankie as Uncle Frankie was a Merchant Marine with a legitimate tattooed Marine Seal on his arm.

I was so happy and proud, and we had a picture taken in front of our private plane with my Uncle Frankie, Uncle Johnny, and my favorite first cousin, Joanie. Joanie was so cute with real long, black-brown hair and high cut bangs as they wore in those days. The picture had her in a ponytail hairdo by her dad, my Uncle John, and me, with a curly permanent and my school bag as I loved school. I remember buying my own school bag at a famous mom and pop candy store named Josie's for which I was very close to them also and loved them. The school bag was made of fine wool and was navy and light and medium blue colors with buckles to loosen the school bag. And guess what? It only cost twenty-five cents for a well-made school bag for which I now know all the men and women made and sewed to perfection on the sewing machines during the war in factories by government standards.

As time went by, I continued to go to school and take care of my grandpop, Uncle Ben and mom, learning to do household chores without having to be told, as I was never forced to do household chores. I learned naturally, watching and staying with my mom and grandpop and uncle. I learned myself how to wash clothes on the old washboards, then we had what you would call a "wringer washer," for which you washed the clothes in an iron round drum, and when the wringer washing machine was done, you took and fed the wet clothes into two rolls that pressed all of the water out of it. It wasn't like the new automatic washing machines you see today that spin the excess water out before putting in a dryer or hanging on a line or allowing to dry flat, if you didn't want your clothes to shrink as an automatic dryer can do this. It wasn't easy. Later, we got an automatic washer for which we had to put in the kitchen as it would not fit through the cellar door opening leading down to the cellar. We had to hook a hose that was in back of the washer to the kitchen spigot to drain the water out of the washing machine as it spun to eliminate the excess water. We could not have an automatic dryer as we had a fairly large kitchen, but not large enough to fit both an automatic washer and dryer, so we still had to hang the clothes on the clothes lines down in the cellar.

When my mom came here from Lithuania with her parents and siblings, as she was growing, there was what you would call clothes lines with pulleys on the roof outside the back bedroom. You would raise the window and hang the clothes one at a time, then work the pulley to move the clothesline so you would have room for the rest of your clothes to hang and they dried outside. I don't know what they did for winter, probably washed and dried enough clothes to carry them through the winter months. Eventually the pulleys rusted and you could not move the pulley lines because of rust from rain and snow over the years. Soon the lines were ruined and just stayed there of no use.

I used to climb out the window when I was little and bring a folding webbed beach chair in the summer and sit on the roof and watch the carnival, which was St. Adalbert's Church and school and was a hop, skip, and jump from our house on the roofs. It was a great old-fashioned scene from our roof as you could see the giant Ferris wheel and all of the happy teenagers and young children enjoying the carnival. A black gentleman, whom we all loved, by the name of George, operated the Ferris wheel every year for St. Adalbert's carnival. It started at 6 PM and ended at 12 AM for two full weeks, Monday to Sunday. It started to get reckless as bad boy teenagers in the neighborhood were getting out of hand. When this happened, like any celebration, the police, or FBI and military squads, would come in and shut everything down and destroy it. I've seen this happen a lot of times, which they will have nothing because of aggressive actions or anything immoral.

It happened with drive-ins, outside movies when you could go to a drive-in movie and watch outside from your car. We have none now because of immoral behavior. There were no drive-in movies in Philadelphia ever as this is a city and there is no land for it. I've seen it happen with clubs, such as night clubs. The now generation is terrible. They like to live in their past with their own crazy styles and want to be accepted, but they're not. You have to have some sense of what is right and what isn't. I've always looked at my past, and I've had a great past doing the best I could. It was very hard for my family and myself, but we made it through and had both good and bad times and were happy. These boys and girls will never really be as happy as I was. They are the worst examples.

Back in time, I actually took tap dancing lessons till I was eighteen-years-old and made a career of it, for which I'll tell you later. We had a school recital for which my dancing teacher choreographed as we became young adolescents about ten- to thirteen-years-old. It was a show with the traditional black top hats, tuxedo costumes, and canes. I always was in the back row, because I was tall and at eleven-years-old I was five foot, seven inches. I also got my menstruation at the age of eleven-years-old, which is considered really young and rare for both today in the 2000s to 2014 as well as when I grew up in the 1950s. So it now was the year 1961, when I was eleven-years-old. Our recital was to an instrumental (which is a song without words), and the name of it was "Calcutta" by Lawrence Welk, from the famous "Lawrence Welk" Sunday TV show.

I thought we were going to tap dance to "Tweedle Dee," which didn't happen. The instrumental "Calcutta" today would be considered corny–not in style–but that is what the school board chose for us as the recital was at James Martin Elementary school, and that is what my tap dancing teacher chose.

When my family and their friends had a huge Christmas party at the Lithuanian Music Hall, the Big Lit Club, I invited my tap dancing friends and said, "Let's put on a show from our recital from what our tap dancing teacher taught us." The routine was fresh in our minds, and this was a spur of the moment idea as I palled around with my tap dancing friends occasionally. There was a Carol Cohen, Robin Kennan, Shelley McRae, Ann Miller, Ann Miller's sister, and Amy Allen, and me. Anne Miller's brother, Joe, in later years, married my tap dancing teacher's second daughter, Lisa. In later years my daughter, Nicole, was the flower girl with my tap dancing teacher's last son, Johnny. Lisa, when she was young, looked like Shirley Temple, a very famous young child tap dancer. Karen choreographed when her three girls were little and made the costumes herself. They were identical to when Shirley Temple did the song, "The Good Ship Lollipop" in a famous movie. The reason that Karen, my tap dancing teacher, did this was because Lisa looked like and had the same persona as Shirley Temple.

Now, to get back to my putting on a show at the Lithuanian Music Hall's Christmas party. The six of us went into the club because my Uncle Frankie was playing piano there for the party. I remember going to his side by the piano and he sang and played a famous song from the days of World War II, "I'll Be Down to Get You in a Taxi Honey." He was great and the crowd cheered and clapped. My uncle really had what you would call "piano hands," as they were long and big to reach the keys easily on the piano.

After my Uncle Frankie was done it was our turn to put on the show. I had to think very quickly. We had a big Wurlitzer jukebox in the club also. I went over and needed to find a song that was about three minutes long like our recital song "Calcutta," as "Calcutta" was not on the jukebox. I found a then very famous song, "These Boots are Made for Walking," by the famous Nancy Sinatra. I quickly thought, "I hope this turns out," as it was an adlib moment to choose the right song quickly as the emcee was announcing us to go on. We lined up, the people clapped as we came on and started tap dancing. Do you know that it began and ended perfectly to my dance teacher's routine to this song? If you are a tap dancer it ended to repeats of the tap dancing step "shuffle toe down." The song "These Boots are Made for Walking" by Nancy Sinatra was great, only we didn't have boots on. Although you could do this routine with cowboy boots with cleats on your tips and heels, which would be great, only we had on tap dancing shoes. The crowd clapped and cheered. I only wish my tap dancing teacher, Karen, had been there to see it. In fact, the school board maybe would have let us use this song.

I may have been twelve to fourtenn years of age for this tap dancing recital. I could just remember at James Martin Elementary school, the grades were kindergarten to sixth, only my last year to go before entering junior high at John Paul Jones junior high school here in Philadelphia. I believe it was on Cedar St., close to Allegheny, about two blocks. I was entering the sixth grade, my last year at James Martin, when they decided to turn it into a nursing school for high school graduates, and for my last year of elementary school, I had to go to Richmond School on the school bus. I believe it was located at Richmond and Belgrade streets, or that vicinity.

We had a great bus driver. His name was Ken. Every day for lunch, we were supposed to go home, but our homes were too far away. So Ken would take us for a ride on the school bus and then we would stop and eat our lunch. He was a dad to all of us. Then we would go back to Richmond school, and Ken would drive us home. Sixth grade at Richmond school, my last year for elementary school, went fast for me. But I missed my original school, James Martin that I started out with. To me there was no reason to change it to begin with. They say that "change is progress." It's not. It just causes more problems for everyone.

Now it was time when I enter junior high school. I went to John Paul Jones junior high school. This was the format here in Philadelphia for public schools. Our first day, I was always happy as I had brand new clothes to wear and we dressed decent, not like the Californians or West Side; we had to wear our skirts below our knees. I began the seventh grade around twelve- or thirteen-years-old. We went to, I think, an auditorium to get our rosters and then we would go home at noon and come back the next day. I was given what you would call a "commercial course." I remember having Filing as a course, along with History, English, Algebra, Geography, and Science. Filing was my favorite out of all of them and I did well in it, because spelling was my favorite subject in elementary school.

It was a great school. My filing teacher's name was Mr. Zim. He was a great teacher and a great man. We also had Glee Club, where there were students that learned to play or succeed from elementary school in music. I only played a flute in elementary school and learned to play a little of the bells, which is like a xylophone.

School was hard for me. Every day my mom would wake me up for school and I would say, "Five more minutes, Mom," and she would let me sleep. Most of the time, after those five more minutes, I would say again, "Five more minutes, Mom," and she would say, "Get up before I throw a bucket of water on you!" And I would get up because my mom would have thrown a bucket of water on me. My mom never hit or abused me, but I never tested her either. I was not allowed to say the word "she" when speaking of someone. I had to say their name. I was not allowed to make fun of anyone either.

I made it through seventh grade with a smart class of pupils, only as time passed it was getting harder for me to catch on to the harder subject of Algebra. My classmates were getting ahead with algebra and I was falling back. I was in a higher section at Jones junior high my first year. It was called Section 7-6. I made a lot of good classmate friends. Their names were June Berger, Harriet Schwartz, Joe Leneghan, Pete Rose, and that's all I can remember name-wise. Then the worst part: when I went to eighth grade, the school wanted to push me up to an academic course with a foreign language study in French. I couldn't do it, because I was like a big sister to my tap dancing teacher's children and would iron their clothes, babysit, clean, wash tons of dishes, plus take care of my mom, uncle and grandpop at my house. So I started bumming school at Jones.

I met a nice beautiful girl by the name of Iris Moore, when I did go to school, in the cafeteria. We always had the best lunches at Jones junior high, for only thirty-five cents. Iris invited me to come over to her house in Fishtown. She lived in the vicinity of Girard and Shackamaxon streets in Philadelphia. I never knew about makeup. Iris showed me mascara, and I put it on for the first time. We had fun together, and for the first time, she put on a record I had never heard of. It was the famous Broadway movie, which is a classical movie today, West Side Story. It was great! I went to Alice's house a lot, and we became very close. She introduced me to her friends, Andrea and Patty; and her sister, Sarah; and her brother, Ben. Here, Iris told me that she, Sarah and Ben were triplets. Her mom was very nice, and she introduced me to her dad, who was a public speaker for his profession.

I loved Fishtown. Iris introduced me to a boy named Mark. We became very good friends, and I would call him every night. As years went on, he was a brother to me and sent my career to the top with his big brother, Bill. I had met his younger sister, Amy, and would stay overnight. I always felt at home. I was the closest to Mark. He had a big family, and their last name was Evans. They lived close to the old St. Mary's Hospital in Fishtown. I will tell you later when I get up to that part how my career started to take off and I made a lot of money for a lot of people that benefitted from it.

Someone once told me that the way our system, government wise, is established, is that it separates you. To me she was right, because from the time you begin school this happens. I think it is good but it is also bad. And there is nothing we can really do about it as life brings so many ups and downs. We all have good and bad in this world and life is hard and we get disappointments, tragedy, travesty and obstacles and distractions. I try to make the best of things, as my mom would say, and avoid people who weren't as successful as me. I like to live in my thoughts of the past. That brings me peace of mind. I miss all of my friends as we have become separated because of the system, and many have also died.

I made a lot of older friends in school when I was in seventh grade and they were in the ninth grade, ready to graduate to go to high school. One girl I met, her name was Janet Carey. She was a plain looking girl like me and very nice. Later in years, after I got married, my husband knew her. I stayed close to Mark Evans. As teenagers, we would go to a luncheonette called the Cambria A.C., located at the corner of Cambria St. and Kensington Ave. I met so many friends there that my husband told me he palled with, but I never saw or knew him then, back in the early 1960s. We had a great crowd and there was one boy by the name of Frankie DeCarlo who could really sing and harmonize.

There was a couple, boyfriend and girlfriend, who were a perfect match. His name was Will McLaughlin and her name was Leslie Flynn. Leslie was a natural beauty. There was Audrey with real long beautiful straight hair, and Bill Mancino. Bill and Audrey were a couple. Bill had an older brother named Joe, who my husband also knew, as they were around the same age. Joe later died from a tragedy. There was Al Brady, and one day we had fun in the luncheonette while the Wurlitzer jukebox was on. We had a ketchup and sugar fight, for fun without hurting each other. Joe had on an olive green long military coat and said, "I feel like I'm in World War III!" One of the boys had ink spot remover in his pocket and accidentally threw it in my eye, and it blinded me temporarily. There was a rather handsome Italian boy with a muscular build that used to have a folded Inquirer or Bulletin newspaper, and he would stand on the corner and swing the newspaper back and forth. His name was Leon DePasqualle.

I never had a boyfriend like the other girls, and Leon took a liking to me as I was a new girl. He wanted to be my boyfriend, but it never worked out. He was nice though. Later in years when I graduated from Jones, I bought an autograph book and he signed a very nice poem in it. He really was a gentleman. There was also a Michael Hughs, who was older, who my husband knew. One night Mark Evans became my boyfriend. I know and remember I was exactly eleven-years-old and he was around sixteen-years-old. Mark could not believe I was only eleven-years-old because, like I said before, I was five foot, seven inches when I was eleven.

I invited Mark and a few friends, Michael Hughs and some of the girls. We had a nice night and played cards. Later, as time went by, Mark brought me to his house to meet his mom and told her when I was eighteen-years-old that then he was going to marry me, but that never worked out. Mark was saying what he really didn't mean and was not ready for marriage. It didn't bother me, and we remained just friends. From the age of eleven to sixteen, I called and talked to Mark every night. When I would call there always was music playing in their house as I could hear it from our Bell telephone. It is the first time I heard a beautiful slow song by a famous singing group named Anthony and the Imperials, called "Just Two Kinds of People in the World." It is the first time I ever heard of this group and my uncle Frankie, who always loved music, used to give me fifty dollars a week for spending money because of all the work I did.

We had a record store in Port Richmond on Richmond St., and I took some spending money with me and went to the record store. All of the records were always filed alphabetically by the singing groups. I found an Anthony and the Imperials album and purchased it for only twenty-five cents as that is all album records cost in those days, along with some forty-five speed records at random for only ten cents. One forty-five speed record said, "Bobby's Girl." I didn't know or hear this song but bought it anyway, along with another song named "Oliver Cool."

For Christmas my mom had bought me a beautiful suitcase type light beige record player. It would open up and you could close it. The sound from a record player like this was not real loud, like all of your music systems today. But I was really surprised and happy and I had a matching light beige cabinet to put the record player on top of. I think my mom, now that I think about it in the year 2014, talked to my Godfather, my uncle John and that's how I got that record player, but she never told me. It was a great surprise. I used to stay by myself in our house as a teen most of the time. I put on the record "Bobby's Girl" and loved it. It was considered "Bubblegum Music" because we girls loved to chew bubblegum and dance. Although you really couldn't dance to the song "Bobby's Girl." It was too fast for a modern line dance Cha-Cha and too hard to keep a beat to a slow dance. It was a great song to watch the female singer who sang it at a club or concert.

I played my Anthony and the Imperials album and every song was great, although the song "Just Two Kinds of People in the World" was not on it. All the songs were hits in the 1960s except for one on this album that never was played on the radio. It was called "Reputation" and it was a beautiful, slow Calypso that teenage girls would love. As the power of Little Anthony's voice was incredible for this song, but never was released, and in the end turned out to be my favorite song of the famous singing group, Little Anthony and the Imperials.

The other forty-five speed record called "Oliver Cool" was a fun song for children, and I loved it as a child and would sing to it. I continued to buy records and picked up one album called "Devil's Gun." It was a great music score, and sometimes you can hear it on WDAS radio station. Also, The Stylistics were a big singing group in my teenage days, and I bought that album for twenty-five cents. My favorite one was called "Hey Girl, Come and Get It," which was never released or played on the radio. It was a slow Calypso.

I graduated from Jones Junior High School and received a beautiful gold and blue small ring that was called a necklace ring. You could not wear it on your finger. It was custom made to be worn as a necklace, not like the girls who have their boyfriends' high school rings, buy a chain and wear it around their necks. There was no fancy graduation party or that I may have known. Summer was here and I was glad school was over until September.

I wanted to go to Mastbaum High School, which was in Kensington next to Port Richmond in Philadelphia. All of the friends I met and got close to were going to Mastbaum, which was considered a technical school. My mom did not want me to go to a technical school, and she wanted me to go to Frankford high school, which was in Frankford, a section in Philadelphia, and was located at Frankford and Wakeling streets. It was a trade school. She would not allow me to go to Mastbaum, and I always listened to my mom's advice as I grew up. It was disappointing for me as I had met so many good friends at Jones junior high.

So I went to my first day at Frankford High School. I had to take the number 60 trolley to Kensington and Allegheny avenues., then the Frankford El to Margaret and Orthodox streets. It was far from my house, and when you got off the el, you had another bus to take, which I think may have been the number fifty-four or walk, and it was two long city blocks. The school was really big, and I remember all of us going in the front door and going again to an auditorium all sat down. There was a girl with long, dark red auburn, soft-curled hair who was next to me. She was friendly and said, "Hi. My name is Theresa." I, at that moment, felt comfortable. I told her my name was Fay, my nickname I always used and all my friends from before knew me by.

We stayed together for the whole day and we received our rosters as we were called one by one from I think our advisor, the same basic procedure we had in Jones. Then we went home. My mom was working as a head waitress for a restaurant chain called Dewey's Famous at 17th and Chancellor streets in downtown Philadelphia, working from 3 PM to 11 PM and getting home every night at exactly twelve AM all eastern standard time. She took the el to Kensington and Allegheny avenues, then the number sixty trolley to the end at Richmond and Westmoreland streets. It was hard for her. She never had any really true friends. They were jealous of her beauty. As time and the years went by, you'll see what I mean and I'll tell you.

So I went to Frankford High and guess what? I started having more friends, so I had twice as many friends from Mastbaum and Frankford. Theresa, my first girlfriend whose full name was Theresa Galdino, lived close to Frankford High on Penn St., at the corner. She had a big home with her parents, brother and little sister. I now felt comfortable and was content with Frankford High. The subjects were hard for me, but I tried to comprehend all that I could, as I always stayed with my mom and family and did a lot of housework for my mom and tap dancing teacher, Karen. I had great teachers and a great advisor. My mom was so happy and proud that I entered Frankford High. I had both good and bad marks from tenth to twelfth grade. We had recess after lunch in school and most of us teenagers smoked cigarettes in the 1960s. Do you know that they let us have smoke breaks outside during recess? I do not approve of smoking, but I am a smoker. We were really lucky. My mom never knew I smoked cigarettes, and I never smoked in front of her. My tap dancing teacher, who was a second mother to me, let me and so did my teachers. I had the best.

One day, entering the eleventh grade, with the same procedure as tenth grade at Frankford High, after reading my roster I went by myself to the girl's lavatory. I don't know what possessed me, but I lit a cigarette inside the toilet stall. A woman, who may have been a teacher or on the school board that I never seen, came in and caught me as she smelled the cigarette smoke. I was the only one in the lavatory, and I was immediately suspended from school that day and could not return until my mom met with the school board. My mom was very calm about it, and I was suspended for about two weeks. My mom had to come to school with me, miss work, and I returned to school. I never did that again. It taught me a lesson as I was lucky that I was able to smoke outside during recess initially with other students.

I really loved Frankford High. I made a new friend. Her name was Susan Patton. She was a beautiful girl, also like a lot of the girlfriends I had. She had pitch black hair, pale skin and always wore a new outfit every day. She never wore the same outfit twice and they were fine tailored clothes. She was very popular as she had a great personality. She and I during lunch breaks would go into the girl's lavatory and dance cha-cha steps for fun. That became my second favorite dance next to tap dancing. After school (I'll take you back to Jones Junior High initially), I would do my homework in front of the television or in me and my mom's bedroom. It was about 3 PM Eastern Standard Time when a dance show called Bandstand came on, and Dick Clark was the host for the TV show. I watched it every day after school, from Monday to Friday. It was a great show and since I was very interested in dancing and still continued to take tap dancing lessons, it gave me an incentive after school in my teenage years.

The dancers were great and the instrumental theme song at the beginning of the show was catchy and drew my interest. They were doing a dance I didn't know about called "The Jitterbug." The TV show was black and white as we did not have color TV yet until I was thirteen-years-old having took this interest before thirteen-years-old. Now that I remember, I was eight-years-old. I found out later in my adult years in the 2000s that the "Jitterbug" dance was originally called "The Bop." As another old saying goes, "You learn something new every day!"

Dewey's Famous restaurant across from the Warwick Hotel, where my mom was head waitress, became very popular. Customers who came in were mostly people who traveled to Philadelphia to stay at the Warwick Hotel, and they began to want only my mom to wait on them. My mom was beautiful and had a great personality with this type of job, waiting on the public. As time went on she waited and became close to a lot of famous movie, TV and baseball stars. They all knew and loved her and wanted only her to wait on them. That is how she became head waitress. They dressed so nice with their uniforms all white with white shoes and hankies in their chest pockets, and on occasions wore artificial corsages. When my mom worked originally for the other famous restaurant chains, Horn and Hardart's andWhite Castle, they dressed basically the same only Horn and Hardart's had beige uniforms and they usually wore corsages with a hanky wrapped around it and tucked in their chest pocket. They were what you would call "high class waitresses," not like some restaurant chains with causal pants and t-shirts that the women wear.

So that is how I had my chance–a lot from my mom in addition to my tap dancing teacher, Karen–to get some noticeability. My mom got me on the TV show, "The Pete Boyle Show," as she became friends with the famous father of Joe Boyle, known for the newer movie version of Frankenstein, with Joe Boyle and Madeline Kahn. I spoke with him, and he told me that I would be hostess for the show and I would have to pick a subject to write about. So I previously found a stray tiger kitten in a snow igloo that the boys in my neighborhood build during a snowstorm, and this kitten was stray and freezing. I brought him home and asked my mom if I could keep him. She said, "Yes," and I named him Tiger. That is the quick idea I came up with for the

Pete Boyle Show. I would go through a sliding board and come out of a house on the set and then other kids followed. It was a lot of fun. My mom waited on so many stars, such as Lucille Ball's mom and son Ricky when he was a child; Vincent Price; all of the famous baseball players of the 1960s; Richie Ashburn and the rest; Phyllis Diller and Bernie Weber from the kids TV show, "The Bernie Weber Show;" Sally Starr from the kids TV show, "The Sally Starr Show;" Chief Halftown; Gene London; Pixanne; Carol Channing; Jayne Mansfield and husband Mickey Hargitay; the rock group "Mothers of Invention;" the Four Seasons with Frankie Valli; Ed Hurst from the famous summer TV show in Atlantic City, "The Ed Hurst Show," which was the summer dance show in place of Bandstand in the winter here in Philadelphia; and the Bandstand dancers went there.

I got a chance with my mom to dance the Pony dance on the Ed Hurst Show by Chubby Checker, and Count Basie was there live with his band. It was great and it was at the famous Steel Pier in Atlantic City, my favorite vacation spot will always and always be on the famous boardwalk about ten blocks from New York Avenue and Kentucky Avenue in the great Atlantic City, New Jersey. You have to take the good with the bad, but who really was behind and discovered Atlantic City and initiated the capital, only they will not admit it, because of the negative side of it, such as gambling, etc. It was Al Laurentis, then came the other famous spots such as Las Vegas. They all were partners together and although it is morally wrong for the wrongdoings that went on, if it wasn't for him we would not have the Atlantic City vacation empire. It was Al Laurentis if you read your history books. So he was bad, but he was good also and powerful, and he paid the price of it. God bless him always.

When I was a little girl I would guess and I'm sure I was 9 years old and in the second grade of the James Martin School. I studied Catholicism and made my Holy Communion at St. George's Parish. My aunt, Jennette, planned an after communion party with my mom to be at my Aunt Jean's house on Livingston St., in Port Richmond. She had a beautiful home. When I came with my mom, my Aunt Jennette was serving Kielbasa, which is Polish. I was raised on Polish food in my childhood days.

There were four gentlemen sitting at the table, for which I did not know them. I was in my Communion dress of white, which was purchased at a famous department store named Cousins on Kensington Ave. These four gentlemen were quiet men. I, later in my adult years, figured out who they were. The first gentleman at the table, now that I remember, was Al Laurentis. The second, his brother, Joe. When I became a dancer and did not have a ride home one night, Joe was the one that took me home and was such a gentleman. He never told me anything either. The third gentleman was John Larentis, Al's brother, and the fourth was Stephen that may have been a very close friend.

My Aunt Jean, whose last name was Marquis, was very good to me and bought me the finest of clothes at the Famous Lit Brothers store. I had a rose pink and navy blue Chinchilla snow suit with a coat and leggings with suspenders. I could vaguely remember now being in a St. Vincent's Home for children, for a short period of time. I think these four gentlemen brought me there temporarily until my grandparents came for me. In the 1950s it was still war and depression and my real dad was in the army. We children of the 1950s were considered the "Baby Boomers" and that phrase was used for the first and only time. You were a Baby Boomer if you were born from 1948 through the early 1960s and were vaccinated on the left arm for measles, smallpox, diphtheria, etc., all in one vaccination shot through a doctor or a nurse at elementary school. My doctor was a man named Dr. Gorski, and he was Polish and our family doctor, who made house calls also as they did in those days, at our house.

Time went by, I was growing up a very popular teenager. I was not very pretty or beautiful and always kept to my studies, along with my tap dancing lessons with Karen. I had met her first cousin Daniele Aidman and Daniele had taught a famous movie and TV star, Brooke Shields, who I think may have also been a model, I'm not sure. Daniele had children of her own, Tommy, Kimberly and Letrice, who were very talented. Tommy was a great singer at a very young age, and Letrice her little girl sang too. Karen and I, still closer, were having a problem with her husband as he was cheating and drinking heavily with her sister-in-law, who was married to my tap dancing teacher Karen's brother, Barry. It tore the whole family, Karen and me apart. We could not believe it, but I think this foolish mistake was from drinking.

Her husband, named Stan, got a very good paying job as he was highly intelligent in his adult years as a machinist with the famous General Electric Company. He did not come home for a very long time and he was also in the Military reserves. I think it was the Navy. Karen and I stayed close as she was my tap dancing teacher, second mom for which I called mom when I was young and she was my mentor. While my mom worked, I'd stay with Karen and her children, who were like my sisters and brothers. We always were together. Karen always sewed on the sewing machine that had a cabinet made of fine wood that her husband bought for her and you could hide the sewing machine in this colonial wood cabinet.

Karen loved the old-fashioned colonial styles of furniture. She got a wooden Cuckoo clock for a gift and every hour the bird would come out and say, "Cuckoo, cuckoo." It drove my dancing teacher Karen nuts and she stopped the bird from coming out as it became annoying. Karen sewed and made all the dance costumes and dresses for her three little girls for special occasions, such as Easter, and they were beautiful. One time though, it was late afternoon, Karen and I were sitting in the dining room, that's where the sewing machine was, and Karen was sewing. Her youngest girl, Christine, was about three years old and learning to go to the bathroom on the big people's toilet, having been trained from the wooden potty chair with the plastic urinal. Christine flushed the toilet, the toilet water pipe broke, and there was a drop ceiling that Stan had installed and the water like Niagara Falls came down on top of my tap dancing teacher's head. Karen was soaking wet, the whole sewing machine and cabinet was ruined and she put her hand to her forehead and said, "Oh God."

The dining room was flooded, I laughed at the surprise when this happened. It would have been great had I had a moving camera for America's Funniest Home Videos TV show. Karen and I mopped the flooded dining room up, and Karen said, "Chrissy," but it was just that the house was getting old and it wasn't Chrissy's fault. Stan came back and took care of Karen, his wife and children, but we really didn't know what was going on with him at the time. He was like a father to me and I admired and respected him because Karen and Stan were an ideal couple. Stan had grandparents that he called Mom and Pop and it seemed strange to me to be his parents as they were much older. One day, when I was exactly thirteen-years-old, I asked my dancing teacher, Karen, "Why does Stan call them mom and pop? They look old to be his parents." That is the day my tap dancing teacher told me a true story I will never forget.

Stan, Karen's husband, had three aunts who were very good to me. Their names were Angie, Dorothy, and Ellen. Karen told me there was a baby sister by the name of Kathleen, for which I never knew of or never saw. Kathleen was Stan's mother. Karen said that when Stan was born with Polio, which affected his lungs, and Stan always sounded like he had a cold when he talked. Karen said that Stan's mother, Kathleen, , was ultra-beautiful naturally. Her and her husband were separated and did not live together for whatever reason I don't know, but Stan's father always gave his wife Kathleen money for their son to raise him. Karen told me one night that Stan's father told his wife Kathleen to meet him under the bridge and, "I will give you money." It was a summer night and Kathleen, his wife, met him there. It may as time went on she would want to be away from him forever but she needed his financial support.

Kathleen had met him under a bridge in Port Richmond, a section in Philadelphia. Kathleen always met him as he was good to her and loved her dearly. This summer night when they met, Stan said to Kathleen, "I love you and if I can't have you nobody will! I don't want anyone to look at you!" He took out a small vial and threw something in her face to make her ugly, not to kill her. But it did kill her, instantly. It was acid and it burned her face and killed her. Karen told me his dad served a thirty-year sentence in the Florida state prison, and Stan was very bitter when he became an adult. Stan was a small child, but he remembered his mom Kathleen. He never ever would want to speak to his dad as an adult or forgive him. Kathleen's three sisters raised Stan, who was their nephew and the people he addressed as mom and pop were his grandparents.

As time went on, before Stan had an affair with his sister-in-law, he was a very good husband and father. His sister-in-law was ugly and didn't look like a lot of beautiful Italian girls, although she was Italian, and married to Karen's brother, Barry. Karen and Stan had three girls close together, about ten months apart, Ann, Lisa, and Christine. When the three girls were little they would always quarrel. Lisa was a little trouble maker and would get Ann and Christine in trouble all of the time. Karen had this superstition that the second child born to a family is always the biggest trouble-maker, but to me that is just a coincidence with maybe her experience.

Karen would also say, which I believe is true, having experienced raising a child, "They're fine until they grow up." My daughter and only child, Nicole," looked similar to Lisa and almost had the same personality. She had brown black hair and looked like my husband until she started bleaching her hair blonde in her adult years. She did look somewhat like me, but only because she bleached her hair blonde–which I disapproved of–when she got married and walked down the Catholic Church aisle at St. Henry's Church with bleached blonde hair. I told you I was born with white platinum hair, and it stayed platinum blonde until after I had her, my daughter, Nicole. My hair started getting darker when I was twenty-three-years-old, and then I started bleaching it. It was extremely oily, and a hairdresser by the name of Gary Christopher–from a popular beauty salon named The Cosmic Hair Studio–advised me that bleaching my hair would control the excess oil, along with other professional hairdressing friends that I had.

To get back to my teenage days, I was either home at my house or at my dancing teacher's house every day and at school. My tap dancing teacher saw I was excelling in tap dancing and put me in her advanced class. Then you had what you would call Twin Tap Cleats that made a double sound and were used by professional tap dancers. I was able to do the harder tap dance steps, called "wings," a "tap step," like the professional male tap dancers. I loved it. That is why I took tap dancing lessons until I was eighteen-years-old. I was seven-years-old when I began tap dancing lessons, and later introduced my daughter when she was a little girl to tap dancing–only she never had a good enough tap dancing teacher like Karen. They were less experienced when it came to tap dancing, but were more professional in ballet, for which my daughter was pretty good at and she wanted to take up. I thought my daughter, having introduced her to tap and ballet, would someday be in plays in addition to another career, but she lost interest and just wanted to be a mom and wife without her name in the Hollywood lights.

So I let my dream of her as a dancer go. But it was a lot of fun all along. She would go into the Anastasia Dance Studio and would not let her dad in, telling him to sit and wait in the car. She was still sucking on a pacifier, but would tell her dad to hold it in the car as she was embarrassed if any of her dancing classmates knew she was still using a pacifier. Then the first thing she would say after dance class to her dad was, "Where is my Jew, Jew?" which was slang for pacifier in a lot of Italian families. She and I got that from a first cousin through marriage on my husband's side who was Italian. Her name was Trixie, short for Nicole.

To go back to my young teen years before the age of thirteen. Stan was getting strict as the girls at a young age were getting out of control and ruining the house. As time went on, the girls were getting bigger and went to St. Adalbert's Catholic School in Port Richmond on Allegheny Ave. It was the most beautiful church in Port Richmond. Then Karen and Stan Bell had their first boy. Karen named him Stan Jr. It was hard for Karen and Stan, and I would stay close to them. I babysat every day, missed a lot of school at that time as I was failing because it was too much school work and I had to take care of my family too, but we were happy. We all worked together. Stan Jr. became my favorite, and I would take him for walks, iron everyone's clothes, clean, and I was happy.

Our house was getting more modern and we were converting from coal to gas heat. I would take Stan Jr. to visit my Aunt Jean's and showed her Karen and Stan's first born son. I would change his diapers and put plastic pants over the diapers as we did not have throwaway diapers in those days. Karen taught me how to put diapers on and to prevent chafing a cream called Desitin first and then Johnson's Baby Powder. I was a big sister. I would take him to his Aunt Ellen's also. As time went on Karen told me he would not eat his baby food, and Karen called me on the telephone to come over to feed him. I came over and fed him, and he ate. He never cried with me. He was a happy child, but as he got to be about six-months-old, he wouldn't go to his mom and would always want to be with me. It was confusing to him because I was always with him, and I was becoming his mother instead of the babysitter or big sister. Finally he went with his mom.

One day Karen had cotton socks that she put on him that would not stay up, so not knowingly put thin rubber bands around the top of the socks then folded them over. He slept in them and the next day when I wanted to change his outfit I took the socks off and noticed a crust around his ankles. Here since a baby's skin is soft the thin rubber bands embedded into his skin. Karen was there and I told her. She immediately gave me surgical scissors to cut the rubber bands out of his ankles. I was successful and got the rubber bands out. His ankles healed but left scars like rings for a long time around the ankles. Thank God, nothing was severe.

Stan Jr. was getting bigger and healthy and quite heavy to carry, but Karen and I were strong, and we took care of the four children while Stan was away on Reserves in the Service. Every night we either played cards, made crafts, or Karen would sew before the flood in the dining room. Karen was also a substitute teacher at James Martin Elementary, but somewhere along the years had forgotten how to spell. The game Scrabble was a big game at that time in the 1960s, but I didn't know about it. For Christmas, the popular games were Chutes and Ladders for young children, Monopoly for families, etc. I don't know why, maybe it is because spelling was my favorite subject, I went to the Hobby Store in my neighborhood where they sold games, projects, educational toys, all name brands. I found the game Scrabble, which was something new that I had never seen, but was attracted to because of the spelling words on top of the box. I purchased it around the age of eleven-years-old and brought it to my house. I read the directions and made pretend there was another playing partner who was playing the game with me so I could teach and play with my friends. I brought the Scrabble game over to Karen's and taught her how to play. I also brought a Webster's pocket dictionary, which I bought at Jones Junior High bookstore with my spending money. I taught my tap dancing teacher the basics of the game and she was very interested in this, what I would call a great learning game. If we weren't sure how to spell a word, we would refer to the dictionary. I was a pretty good speller and most of it was done by memory, so naturally I always won.

We played every single night and Karen was becoming good at learning to spell from playing the game. Karen always would tell us to practice our tap dancing steps as we got better, and she became so absorbed as a dance teacher, wife, mother, and our mentor that the Scrabble game was helping her to spell, of what she may have forgot, from her childhood days, when she was growing, since she was a young, beautiful mother. Karen always kept us busy and everyone was happy. We all loved Stanas; he was a dad to all of us growing up in our neighborhood. I had a great childhood and teenage years, and tap dancing was the beginning of my happy life.

Time went by and Stan Jr. was growing into a young boy now. He was very close to his dad. Karen had a dad whose name was Leo, and he had a brother who was a dentist on Richmond St. Stan Jr. was losing his baby teeth now, and around the age of nine-years-old he had a terrible toothache. Karen's father's brother, whose real name I did not know, did not pull Stan Jr.'s tooth. His father tied a string to cellar doorknob and his loose tooth. He opened the door, then closed it quickly, and Stan Jr.'s tooth fell out. I think his dad was giving him his first lesson in pain, even though Stan Jr. had an uncle who was a professional dentist named Doc and Karen and Stan's children called him Uncle Doc.

Time went by again. Very soon Karen gave birth to another son, for which she named John after her dad, and we called him Johnny. I was getting older and had a new boyfriend named Joe. His full name was Barry Cilino. He was full-blooded Italian and Karen and Stan liked him. Barry's dad was a shoemaker and made all of Sally Starr's boots. Barry and his parents had a row home next to a bar at Torresdale Avenue and Margaret St. The name of the shoemaker shop was "Chuckwagon Joe's," and Barry and his family lived above it. Today it is a Chinese nail salon and there are too many of them in my opinion, a total waste of your money.

Barry stayed close to his parents and helped in the shoe repair shop with his dad. I too would help when his parents would go on vacation, as people would come to pick up their repaired shoes. Joe would come to my house every day after he got another job in a shirt factory, after work. I would tell him when I was babysitting at Karen and Stan's and he would visit me, then go home and I would stay overnight at Karen and Stan's. As the youngest of all of Karen and Stan's children was Jimmy, I wasn't close to him, because as a young boy he was strange and devious. He was unruly and a troublemaker like Lisa.

But I was older now and was in high school. My last year was coming up and I was flunking gym. I had 90 makeups to do or I could not graduate, and I said to the teacher, "How can I do this in one month?" It was impossible. I told her I was going to quit and she threatened me by saying, "You won't get your diploma unless you come after work to make up your gym." So I went home and told my mom, "I wanna quit school because of this." She said that it was okay, and I went and got my working papers in September of 1968. But guess what? My senior prom was all planned, and I bought a beautiful emerald green full with a crinoline slip attached. It was an umpire evening gown. Umpire dresses, evening gowns, and wedding gowns were the style and fashion of the late 1960s that I remember. I purchased my evening gown at a bridal salon in Kensington on Kensington Ave. The top part of my gown had sequins scrolled through it with a sleeveless top. I asked the bridal consultant if I could have rhinestone spaghetti straps made and she said yes. I came back and saw how beautiful the dress designer who was a female made the rhinestone spaghetti straps on the gown. It was beautiful. I chose a plain, long white, satin evening coat to go with my gown. It was the length of my evening gown and had a small satin bow with rhinestones in the center to close the evening coat.

Barry rented a black and white tuxedo. The jacket was white and the pants were black, and he bought me white orchids. So even though I never received a high school diploma we still went to my Frankford Senior High prom at the Sheraton Hotel in Center City. They served a chicken dinner. They were chicken legs with bones. And to tell you, I did not know how to cut the chicken, so I did not eat that evening because I wanted to pick the chicken legs up and eat them with my hands. But I knew I might get my gown dirty with chicken grease, so I didn't eat the dinner. I just sat and after everyone was done eating we went down to a huge, beautiful ballroom. It was highly elegant and planned by the Frankford High school board. We danced to classical music with a live band and we did the waltz. It was very nice. I forgot to mention my hairstyle.

Karen lived close to a beauty shop on Ontario St. The name of the beauty shop, lit up in neon lights, was "Leona's." Before the senior prom I looked in our Bell telephone book and called Leona's to make a hair appointment. I asked how much it would cost and she told me fifteen dollars for a shampoo and style. So my appointment was made and on the day of the prom I went to the hairdresser's. When I came in my hair was already cut as I learned to cut my own hair from Karen. I loved to do a set and style on my own hair and learned from hairstyle magazines that I would buy. I think then, they were twenty-five cents or one dollar and twenty-five cents. I told the hairdresser, Leona, that I wanted a page boy fluff, and she did my hair beautifully. I had hairspray by Caryl Richards sprayed on that was in a beautiful pale lavender can and the scent was beautiful. Later in years I found out it had the scent of Nina Ricci's famous signature scent, "L'air du Temps." My whole prom outfit with my beautiful hairdo by Leona was perfect. I wore very little makeup, only mascara that my friend, Iris Moore, had taught me how to apply with Noxema liquid makeup. I wore no lipstick or other jewelry.

My mom was working that evening at Dewey's and told me beforehand to come to the restaurant before Barry and I went to the prom. Barry came for me in the original Philadelphia yellow taxi cab with checkers on the taxi cab. We went to Dewey's and Barry and I went inside as the yellow cab waited for us outside. My mom was so happy and proud as she showed me off to all of the other waitresses and staff. Barry and I left for my senior prom and it was a beautiful, happy, memorable evening that I'll cherish forever.

We had my senior prom in May of 1968. It was at the famous Sheraton hotel in downtown Philadelphia. We danced that waltz for which today's generation would say it was corny as I remember thinking that way with my mom's generation, but actually you felt like debutants and I was happy that our principal, vice principal and the school board planned this elegant evening and I wish I had them today, but they are too old or have passed away.

My boyfriend Joe's senior prom was planned by Father Judge Catholic High School for boys. That was even better. Today's generation would love it, if they only would get off of the hip hop dancing and the rap music. It's not dancing at all. At Joe's senior prom, I wore a peachy pink straight gown with a kick pleat in the back, which is a slit so you can walk or dance, and two-and-one-half Rayon silk dyed shoes from the famous Baker's shoe store on 11th and Chestnut streets. I think it was on 11th and Chestnut streets. Joe got me a wristlet corsage, and he wore the traditional tuxedo suit, white jacket, and black straight pants. No bell bottoms. It was at the Falcon House in downtown Philadelphia and we had a very famous singing group Lee Andrews and the Hearts and you would love the next group of today's generation as occasionally they play this party song by the Artistics, called "Ain't' Nothing but a Party," or it might be listed as "House Party" by the Artistics. We danced only one famous dance to that song, and it's a hard dance to do. You don't need a partner, but you need a lot of room not to bump into each other and I don't know the name of that dance, but it was popular like the jitterbug, Bristol stomp, the new cha-cha line dance, etc., if you could do that dance to the song "House Party." Not many boys or girls could do it. You would have to be the Nicholas Brothers, who were famous dancers, or close to them, but never could dance like Michael Jackson. Remember what I told you before, you learn from the "granddaddies" and "grandmoms" of music and dance. You can't make up something new. You are only a follower of them and you are just improvising, which means you're trying to make your own individual style or make it look fancier from simple basic dance steps. Watch an old black and white movie before color TV came and watch the Nicholas Brothers. You'll wish you were there as you felt the same way with Michael Jackson and the Jackson Five. We'll all miss them and the now generation can only try to carry the tradition of tap dancing, like the Nicholas Brothers and their famous movies.

I quit school a month before graduation in my last year of high school at Frankford and got my working papers. My mom told me about a job agency by the name of Snellen & Snellen here in Philadelphia. I went there and the interviewer asked me what I could do. I told him I had a commercial course in junior high school, which carried over to high school, and I could type sixty words per minute and do filing. He found me a job working for a credit office for the famous JC Penney company. I went there and was hired, started working at fifty dollars per week for forty hours a week. I typed envelopes, which were names and addresses for JC Penney's bills.

I had an instructor by the name of Mrs. Joan Albright. She was a beautiful lady but very strict and business-wise. She showed me a machine, which was like a large projection machine with names and addresses. I really didn't know of this system but I think I typed names and addresses from these cards that were shown what I think was a projection machine. I was happy. I had my own typewriter and would type envelopes all day and every day. That was my job.

My first girlfriend, Vivian, for which I was very close to, needed a job. She had gotten the job through me working for the JC Penney credit offices under my boss Mrs. Albright. Vivian and I usually came home together. One day when we were off on the weekend, Vivian wanted to bleach her brown hair blonde. I had natural platinum blonde hair. Vivian bought a blonde hair kit. I read the directions and started to bleach her hair. You had to keep it on for, I think, forty minutes or more. We did this at my house and the time was up to rinse the bleach solution out. When we went into the bathroom my Uncle Frankie had just got done going to the bathroom. When I started rinsing Vivian's hair, between the smell of ammonia from the hair bleach and my uncle going to the bathroom, we were gagging over the old bathtub. But we were laughing at the same time too. It was all rinsed out but looked like a fire plug, engine red color instead of blonde. We waited until it dried, and it looked awful. I told Vivian, "You are going to have to go to a professional hairdresser, as you could not re-bleach your hair again right after." In the meantime we still had to go to work, and Vivian had to work with this fire engine red hair. I really don't know where she went but as time passed she found a hairdresser and her new bleached blonde hair looked nice on her–although personally I thought she looked better with her natural dark brown black hair, but Vivian wanted to be a blonde and remained a blonde. And guess what? As years went on Vivian became a professional hairdresser, a licensed professional hairdresser. And I'll never forget that story.

I was still working at the JC Penney credit office at 6th and Walnut streets, and was close to my first boyfriend, Mark Evans. We became platonic friends and he was very nice to me. I would call him and we would talk every single night. He was like a brother to me. He had a big family and I would go to where he lived in Fishtown on weekends. I remember he had an older sister whose nickname was Daisy. I didn't know her real name and Mark had a younger sister named Eileen. This relationship with Mark and his family started when I was eleven-years-old, and continued for a long time. I was still taking tap dancing lessons all along, even when I was working for the JC Penney credit office here in Philadelphia. Mark had an older brother named Paul, and Paul was their mom's favorite. He was very conservative, highly intelligent, and a perfect gentleman. When I was eleven-years-old and met Mark, he was the one who could not believe I was eleven because I was so tall.

Now as time passed I was sixteen, still tap dancing, and Mark and I loved music. There always was music in their house also as mine. I remember when I was talking on the phone from my house to Mark's on our then Bell corded black telephones, there was a slow song that Mark had on with his family. I didn't know the song but it interested me, and I later heard the exact same song on my uncle Frankie's white Zenith radio, a very famous name for TVs and radios. The song was "Just Two Kinds of People in the World" by the famous Little Anthony of the famous Anthony and the Imperials singing group. I went to the record store at either the age of eight-years-old or eleven-years-old and bought an Anthony and the Imperials album for twenty-five cents. Can you believe it? Albums were only twenty-five cents and single records only ten cents. "Just Two Kinds of People in the World" was not on it, but all the famous songs the group sang as time went on were. One on that album became my favorite. It was called "Reputation" and had a cha-cha beat, but it was never heard on the radio although I think a lot of girls or ladies would love to hear. It was a beautiful song sung by Little Anthony. His other famous songs in the 1960s on this album were "I Miss You So," I'm on the Outside Looking In," etc. I can't remember the other songs on this album. The album cover was dark midnight blue with a hot pink circle around "Little Anthony & the Imperials."

As time passed I met a lot of friends in Fishtown and had fun growing up. Somehow Mark's brother must have known that I was taking tap dancing lessons. I was able to pick up practically any dance just from watching the dance TV shows on TV, such as Bandstand, which I taught myself, the famous then line dance, the Stroll, the new cha-cha and line dances from the famous Phil Goldman's TV show, "The Discophonic Scene," for which I forget the names of the line dances but they would do them to particular songs. Mark's brother Billy told me, "Do you want a dancing job?" And I said, "Yes." This became the big start of my dance career. I did not tell anyone about it.

I received an agent by the name of Marvin. I had met him and he was a nice little guy and a perfect gentleman. He was a booking agent for talent. I did not have any kind of a dance costume then. There was a new kind of style in the 1960s called Go Go girls. As I said, I did not have a dance costume so I had to think very quickly as I got my first booking from Marvin at a bar in Delaware County, out of Philadelphia. It was far. I had a medium turquoise colored two-piece bathing suit that I used maybe one time for swimming, whether it be at home in Philadelphia at the outdoor pools, or when I went on vacation with my mom in Atlantic City, NJ. I went to the club in Delaware County with my bathing suit on and clothes over it in a yellow taxi cab. The boss was very nice and I think his name was Joey. I danced to songs and got paid very well from my booking agent and boss.

I quit my job at the JC Penney credit office as it was paying only fifty dollars a week for forty hours a week, and I wasn't getting any kind of raise and didn't ask for it. I told my mom and my Uncle Frankie. I then got another booking from Marvin, my booking agent, and the name of the club was called the Gaslight, right across the street from the famous WDAS Radio station, for which I did not know then. My bosses were Mr. and Mrs. George Suriano, or, Rhonda and George. Rhonda was a high class lady with style and looked like an Elizabeth Taylor, only she had natural light auburn hair. George and Rhonda were the owners of the club. George was very high class with pitch black hair and a goatee and always was dignified and he was strict, clean cut, finely dressed and an excellent business man.

When I got there, maybe around 8:30 PM as the club opened at 9:00 PM, I heard the boss and owner Bill say that one of the waitresses got in a car accident. I didn't think anything of it then, but later as time went by I did, but never questioned it.

The Gaslight was a small club but very high class with a small stage for dancers about the size of a small bathroom or closet but made a great appearance with a full-length mirror the size of the small stage and was an attention getter. The walls had dark red velvet flocked wallpaper with electric glass candle sconces and the name "The Gaslight" was a perfect name for this atmosphere and club. There was a long bar, an aisle to walk, and the booths were next to the aisle. There was a kitchen in the back. There was a jukebox for which I could pick records to dance to. There were other dancers when I got there and I felt comfortable. People started coming in when the club opened at 9 PM, Eastern Standard Time right here in my hometown of Philadelphia, PA.

I had bought a ballet leotard dance costume at the famous Baum's, I would say for show people, in black that ballerinas use for practicing ballet. As a little time went on after the club opened there was a chubby man who wore a black leather patch on his right eye and it scared me as I had never seen anything like this and to me, from the old black and white movies that I had seen when I was younger, I thought he was a gangster. He grabbed my hand, and it scared me even more. I went toward the stage as I had already picked my songs to dance. The go-go girls, including me, had to pick three records and dance to three songs, then the next go-go girl would dance. I went on stage after having met this man with the black leather patch.

I danced to the songs and records and ad-libbed on stage. I always loved the Motown music for which I grew up with and looked at the selection of songs such as the famous song of the 1960s, "My Girl," by the famous group and my favorite singing group, the Temptations. I danced the, considered then, new cha-cha dance, which was a line dance but I ad-libbed and did this dance by myself on stage to "My Girl."

I was booked practically every night, practically by my agent Marvin and content. There was a chef by the nickname of Buckwheat, who made the best food and we were able to eat on break if we wanted and we paid for it like the customers. It was always crowded and a happy environment. Buckwheat would tell jokes and he was quite a celebrity. One time, as time went by, my bosses needed me to waitress one night, as it may have been one of the waitress's night off. So another go-go girl, by the name of Jan, and I wore our Baum's black ballet leotard dance costumes.

I went over to one of the booths and there was an older lady with a younger lady and I asked, "Can I take your order?" They ordered the famous Gaslight hamburger with french fries. I went into the kitchen and gave the order to Buckwheat. I served the ladies their drinks and waited for their food order to be cooked. I went back into the kitchen, got their order, and brought it to their booth. When the ladies opened up the roll as I was ready to leave and serve someone else, I overheard the older lady said, "Where's the hamburgers? Here, the traditional tomato and lettuce were on the rolls, but not the hamburgers." So I came back and took their plates to get the hamburgers. When I went in the kitchen, Buckwheat was laughing hysterically with the other chefs. I told Buckwheat, "There's no hamburgers on the rolls," and he put them on. Here, Buckwheat was just playing a little harmless joke, like you would see in a black and white, "Laurel and Hardy" movie, and the older woman and younger girl got their famous Gaslight hamburgers.

The Gaslight club at City Line Ave and Monument Rd., across from the WDAS radio station was doing very well and my boss, Bill, wanted to open up a bigger club at City Line and West Chester Pike in Delaware County. I worked with my agent Marvin and was booked to go-go dance there. It was farther from where I lived in Port Richmond, but I was very happy go-go dancing. All of the go-go girls, waitresses, bartenders and chefs all got along. I got directions on how to get there when it was called PTC, which means Pennsylvania Transportation Company, which is now called Septa. I don't think Septa's style of uniform clothing has the high class style as when it was called PTC. The women to me look like police officers. Why the name and styles were changed is something I don't know and to me it looks worse, and I wish it was in reverse like those days as I remember.

So I got my directions to go to my boss's new club. I took the number sixty trolley from the trolley stop at Richmond and Emery streets, to Kensington and Allegheny. The famous Horn and Hardart's restaurant was right next to the El stop, which is now where Walgreen's is. When I was going to dance, it was early evening when I would get off the sixty trolley and the handsomest guys would be harmonizing songs as what is known as doo wop. They dressed finely all the time, and that was their hangout. The famous actor you might have heard of by the name of Michael Keaton, who did one popular movie that I know of called "Mr. Mom," a comedy, is from Kensington here in Philadelphia; like Sylvester Stallone who is famous for Rocky, which are movies about fighters which are called boxers and considered an extremely dangerous sport.

After the sixty trolley I took the El, which is a train. It was a long ride as I had to go to the last stop, which was 69th and Market streets, another famous Philadelphia area for which I really didn't know of too much, but it was a great area and I could remember seeing a lot of lights that looked like the old famous movie houses. I then took a Red Arrow bus, which took me to the second Gaslight club. It was bigger and beautiful with the same atmosphere as the first Gaslight, with a nice bigger stage and the bar connected below the stage and around it with a small dance floor. My boss Bill named the two clubs. The one across from the famous WDAS radio station was called the Gaslight East and the new, bigger one was called the Gaslight West and was real high class. Bill was a serious, strict businessman and directed everyone. Famous singers of then in the 1960s would frequent the Gaslight East, such as Rhythm & Blues singer Bobby Womack. I loved his style and music.

So I came to work on my first night. I only knew of the Motown, or what is known as Rhythm & Blues songs, when I grew up to really want to go-go dance to. There was a change in music when the Beatles came for which later in my teenage years I really didn't like that much and only followed it because it was a fad. To me, the beginning of the Beatles music as I think in my adult years, is ridiculous when I hear the song "She Loves You," but everyone starts at the bottom with any type of profession and the Beatles are famous. I will always love the song "This Boy," sung by Ringo of the Beatles. The go-go girls at the Gaslight, some of them danced to this type of music, for which I did not like at all, and they could not dance as they didn't know how to.

When I would go to the jukebox to play my three songs to dance to, I was always looking for the Motown music to dance to and I didn't know this new, what they called Pop Explosion music. To me it was very strange to dance to and these go-go girls who were into this music could not dance at all and it had to be degrading to my high class boss, Bill. But the girls were nice and we all got along. They danced to their type of music and I danced to my music. It wasn't easy when we danced, because we had to pick three songs to dance to right away to go up on stage as customers were there to see the go-go dancers, eat, have a few drinks and enjoy themselves. Couples would come in as well as single persons. Most of the time I ad-libbed my dancing to the music and dances I learned from Bandstand and the Discophonic Scene TV shows which were very famous then in the 1960s and I miss it today, and you will too.

The waitress my boss Bill was talking about, who had gotten into a car accident the first night I danced at the Gaslight East, was not heard back yet and I didn't know who she was. I continued to work at the Gaslight West and another waitress was probably off and Bill asked me to waitress. There was a beautiful waitress that looked like a beautiful barmaid to me. She had on a darker purple Baum's danskin leotard with a zipper in the front that was new looking to me from the traditional ballet danskin leotards I had always seen. The beautiful barmaid waitress had bleached blonde hair and it was styled in a famous 1960s hairdo called French curls, with a French twist. I heard Bill call her by the name of Patty. I loved her style and followed her when I waitressed this one night. I had seen her right side of her beautiful face. I waitressed that evening following her then I had seen the left side of her face. It was scarred with a long curve and cross-like slashes across the long curved scar.

I didn't think anything of it then in the 1960s and never asked about it. It scared me, as it did the night I met the man with the black patch over his right eye, when I thought about it at that moment, having seen this beautiful bar maid waitress named Patty. But I never questioned or asked about it. I idolized her style and went and bought a purple danskin along with another lighter marine blue sleeveless danskin that had a tie around the waist like hers. She was my idol and best example out of anyone for the Gaslight clubs. The other go-go girls looked sloppy and trashy to me. They would have danskin bodysuits that looked too small for them as the sides of the danskin legs were raised close to their hips, real high. My first danskin bodysuit fit me like it should have at the top of the legs, and I did not want to look trashy like them. They were ugly, I could not dance, and they did not fit my boss Bill's "high class" persona. So I began following Patty for the way I wanted to dress when I go-go danced.

I go-go danced to Motown songs that were famous in the 1960s, such as "My Girl" by the Temptations–my favorite singing group of then and today–and a lot of Calypso and cha-cha songs that were famous as I loved that rhythm of beat in music. It was easy for me to go-go dance to as it wasn't real fast, like some go-go dance music then. I also danced to the famous James Brown songs when go-go dancing was so popular then. I ad-libbed to the Fifth Dimension singing group, to one of their famous songs, "Aquarius," which started out slow then got fast. I used to watch a famous TV show in the 1960s every week called "Hawaii Five O" when I wasn't go-go dancing.

One night when I was working at the Gaslight East, across from the WDAS radio station, I seen the instrumental song Hawaii Five O and decided to try this to ad-lib my go-go dancing to. It was a fast instrumental song that I liked and I didn't have time to practice go-go dancing or make up a routine at home, as I was tired and took care of a lot at home with my tap dancing teacher Karen, her home and my family's home where I grew up. So I put this instrumental song Hawaii Five O and did a famous dance from the 1960s, for which I don't even know the name of the dance. And the older teenagers that I had seen, did it to a slower paced song, like a slower Calypso or cha-cha song. I would say that would have to be my personal funny go-go dance, and it turned out alright. If the famous singers were here today that I grew up dancing to their styles, they would really laugh as it was a fast song and I didn't know what to do at the moment, ad-libbing to the Hawaii Five O television theme song.

Both Gaslight clubs were highly successful because of my boss, Bill. Refined clientele frequented there to eat and have a few drinks. The clubs were open for lunch hours up until 2 AM every day, except Sunday as I remember. And I was proud and happy to be a go-go girl of the 1960s, and it was all from learning tap dancing and I was an original. I danced to a song by the famous group Smokey Robinson and the Miracles called "You Must Be Love." It was a slow cha-cha beat, and I ad-libbed to it and received many claps and cheers. I never took my clothes off to dance nude like a lot of trash, although Bill said male customers are looking to see nudity and I was not going to do that. I, and the other great dancing go-go girls, didn't need to. We were very talented, danced well and my boss as well as mayor Frank Rizzo of the 1960s, who was a tough police commissioner, also would not allow such trash. I was happy that he was the mayor then, and later on in my adult years after I was married.

I had met mayor Frank Rizzo when it was announced on TV that he would be at the municipal court building here in Philadelphia, as he was the mayor then in the 1960s; and I, in the 1990s, was working in a new profession for the perfume industry, promoting famous perfumes in famous department stores such as Strawbridge & Clothier, Saks Fifth Avenue, Lord & Taylor, and my favorite and the most beautiful department store in the whole wide world, John Wanamaker's–which is now named Macy's and still keeps the famous John Wanamaker tradition and high style, and flamboyancy, that I will always treasure and love. I can remember when Strawbridge and Clothier wanted to be like the John Wanamaker department store but never could, as Strawbridge & Clothier was traditional in a sense that drew common customers for common tastes. Strawbridge & Clothier purchased it for a short time, and through all the hardships that the Wanamaker department store was facing, it was best Macy's purchased it as Macy's had a similar image that originated in New York City, New York. Macy's was famous in the 1960s for sponsoring the famous televised Macy's Thanksgiving Day parade here in Philadelphia on New Year's Day with the Macy's parade going on in New York City, New York, while the famous Mummers Parade was here in Philadelphia and also televised. It was always and still is today up to the year 2015 a great, happy time, and people come from all over to celebrate. It is always policed to the highest standards. I am so proud of the city that I was born in, the first city of the United States, Philadelphia, PA.

I continued to go-go dance at the Gaslight clubs. I met a lot of nice people and very important people too, for which I never knew they were important, as they never bragged about their success and as my uncle Frankie would say to anyone who bragged, "Stop your bragging." And he was really something to brag about.

As time went on a go-go girl by the name of Karen, like my tap dancing teacher Karen, was very recognized for her dancing and beauty. She and I would go out after work to private after-hours clubs. There was a famous nightclub in Springfield, PA, close to the Gaslight West, called the Sportsman's Club. It was also a great nightclub. There were large lighted pictures of race horses racing at the races and the Sportsman's Club stayed open until dawn, around 6 AM, Eastern Standard Time. Karen was go-go dancing and going to college at the same time to study to be a model in fashion. She became a famous local Philadelphia model for Karen McFadden clothes for the John Wanamaker department store. She had ultra-beauty with brown/black hair and wore a Cleopatra hairstyle with bangs and her long hair when I knew and remember her.

Later in my married years, I had gone to a nightclub in Philadelphia called the Classroom with my husband in the 1980s and saw her and was so happy to see her. I later told my husband of her modeling success with Karen McFadden for the John Wanamaker department store and she still kept her beauty and style. She was famous for dancing with a flesh colored Baum's dance leotard under a strobe light she was incredible when she danced to a slow song by a singer, Esther Phillips called "Solitary Woman."

There was another go-go girl who was unique by the name of Estelle, who danced with snakes of all sizes. She was not a beautiful girl but very nice and she was talented with her dance act. She had a boyfriend named Elliott who always smoked a pipe and had a persona like Peter from the singing trio Peter, Paul & Mary and even looked like Peter. He wore a goatee which is a man's beard and was the nicest guy and always stayed close to Estelle. Elliott was what I would call a beatnik before the days of the hippies. Elliott and Estelle made the perfect couple. One time Estelle asked me to hold an Inquirer newspaper cloth bag with one of her snakes before she went on stage as she was getting ready to perform her dance routine. I couldn't wait until Estelle came.

One day, during a lunch hour at the Gaslight West, I was booked by my agent Marvin to dance and went to work. It was quiet and the club was not open yet. When I went in the club, no one else was there yet. Only Patty, the barmaid waitress, and me. My boss Bill may have been in the kitchen or his office or didn't come in yet at the Gaslight West club, but I only seen Patty there that afternoon. None of the employees were in yet. I went to the bathroom to check my appearance in the mirror and came out. I was standing alongside of the bar when a husky man with blonde hair that I never seen before came in with a very mad look on his face. He started chasing Patty across the stage and in her soft voice was screaming and running away on the stage. I just stepped back. Patty ran off the stage and I think flew out the back door, and I'm pretty sure it may have been her husband. As years went on, in my adult years when I was married, I remembered Patty was the waitress, my boss, Bill, was talking about on my first night go-go dancing at the Gaslight East, who said one of the waitresses got into an accident. Now, after maybe thirty years of never asking about it or questioning it, I knew how this beautiful barmaid waitress, Patty, got the scar on the left side of her beautiful face. Plastic surgery really was not heard of in the 1960s as you hear of it today. And do you want to know something? Patty was the most beautiful, with the way I had seen her and later on when I noticed the scar, left untouched. That is something that I'll always remember. She was my best example of beauty in the go-go dancing world of the 1960s. She was original at the Gaslight Club. And if I had the chance to see her today I would thank her for the success I had in the go-go dancing working world of the 1960s. She was clean like the rest of the go-go girls I associated with and we didn't take our clothes off to lure men.

We were really talented. I realized in my adult years, from the past, that bad books with dirty photographs and also of the movies you that see that are not censored, are not censored because of the Comcast cable corporation, for which I blame everything since they introduced paid TV to homes. It is terrible. There is no censorship like years ago in TV and now up to the year 2015; it is trash from the Comcast TV corporation, and they know they are a disgrace with no morals. The damage is done, and they cannot do anything to reverse it. I blame Jeffrey Lurie, whom it was said that he was the owner of the Comcast corporation, and he did nothing to make it a cleaner corporation. Thank God that when I was growing up, there was the McCarthy Era, with strict censorship. It only perverts everyone's minds. Go-go girls when I danced in the 1960s were considered immoral because of past trashy dancing. Again I thank–who is now deceased–mayor and police commissioner, Frank Rizzo. But believe me, after he passed away that is when all the dirty, trashy night clubs started again because we never had a tougher mayor after that to stop it. And people just closed their eyes and let it happen again, and we did not want it.

I went to work at the Gaslight West for a lunch hour that I was booked for by my agent, not knowing it would be my last day. I went to tidy myself up in the bathroom, but I was exhausted from all of the dancing I had done previously, in addition to taking care of my family and my dancing teacher Karen's family with household chores and babysitting the sisters and brothers that I had come to love and they loved me. When I came in to the Gaslight West that afternoon, there was one man sitting at the bar. There was no one else, only my boss, Bill, this man, and myself. He was a fine looking, husky man with a fine tailored black camel hair or wool coat as we would call it. I overheard this man say to Bill, "Who is this Felicia," which is my real name. I went on stage to dance and I was exhausted, but I danced to the usual three songs that we go-go girls would choose to dance to.

When I came down from the stage, Bill said, "Fay," which is my nickname, my mom's real name, to tell me to leave. Wait till I tell you the rest of this of what happened before this day. I did not question Bill and left to go home. The man I had seen looked familiar, as years and years passed, but then I did not know who he was, and that was in the 1960s.

I talked to my agent, and I got booked for dancing at the nightclub closer to my house in Port Richmond, in Philadelphia PA. It was at 5th St. and Wyoming Ave. and the name was Joey's Lounge. I can't remember the exact number of the second trolley that I took to get there, but the first was the number sixty trolley. The second trolley was great because it stopped right in front of Joey's Lounge. I had met the owner, who had impeccable taste like my boss Bill, and his name was Joey. His full real name was Joey Martino. He was the nicest guy and very nice to me, and I felt comfortable. I was ready to dance and content.

There was a jukebox close to the entrance and had good songs that I liked to choose from. There was a long bar and a small wooden low stand to dance on. There were a few customers or patrons there. I danced and was happy and was paid very well. In the beginning weeks of dancing at Joey's Lounge there were not too many people coming in, but as time went on people may have like the way I danced and more people, men and women, were coming in. My boss Joey asked me if I knew any good dancers and I said yes, as Joey wanted to build up the nightclub. I had danced on a famous TV dance show in the 1960s called the Hy Lit Show. I was a professional dancer and paid for the TV show as well as all the nightclubs I worked for. To be paid in "money" or money you have to be a professional and that goes for any job if you do it well.

There's an old saying or phrase, "If you can't do the job well, don't do it at all," and that is so true, even today in the year 2015. I tried to put my heart and soul into anything I did, to benefit myself as well as others. My closest go-go dancer girlfriend was Tina, known as Baby Jane for her dance act. Her real name was Tina Evans, who looked exactly with the same talent of the famous Tina Turner. So I told Tina about the new nightclub, Joey's Lounge. She was happy and excited that we had a new nightclub to dance at and we would be together. On the Hy Lit dance TV show I danced with two gentlemen who were clean cut guys, and they were considered go-go boys on the show. It was great. There was nothing obscene or dirty on the Hy Lit TV show. Their names were Petey and Philip. I told them and they were eager to dance as they were also great dancers and they could make more money in addition to the Hy Lit show.

I had gotten a rest from dancing and housework after the Gaslight Club and was ready to dance again. My boss Joey was grateful and I introduced him to Tina, Petey, and Philip. We all had our own individual styles of dancing and were ready to start. Joey's Lounge was now always fully packed, especially on Friday and Saturday nights. Promotional record men were coming in and asked what songs we wanted for the jukebox. We got what we wanted, and the promotional men were happy and paid very well also.

Everyone loved Joey. He was congenial, which is kind, and people were happy. I can't remember all of the songs I asked for at Joey's, but I remember one song I requested for my break to hear, as you always had to keep the jukebox playing music. I asked for a slow song that I always loved. The first time I heard it was at another girlfriend's house, Betty Gregory, when we were younger, and it was called "The Wind," by a famous singing group called the Jesters. I loved this song when I was about eleven-years-old and remembered it. It was a song with no instruments, just singing. I even used to sing it by myself when no one was around, and I should have gone to singing school in addition to dancing school because I would have made it as a singer also, but it would have been too much for me, taking care of my family and Betty's family. So I just kept it to myself and sang alone. I was content with my life, just dancing and being with my family, my dancing teacher Betty and her family. You can't, as a human being, do it all, or maybe you have done it all but your body slows down from exertion and you need a rest, sometimes a long rest.

Joey's Lounge in Philadelphia, PA was a success. We had a lot of nice people frequent the club. There also was a pool table through an archway and the men played pool. I never really went into the pool room. I just stayed by the bar when I danced and on break I would sit at the bar.

One night I was selecting my songs to dance to. I had something different to wear from the usual go-go girls in my days of go-go dancing in the 1960s. I purchased it at a famous store in Philadelphia called the Cameo Shop. I also went downtown, under the El, where there were a lot of businesses. I didn't sweat too much when I danced. I would control my sweat so my face and my hair would not be soaking wet as I would look horrible and did not have time to play around with my face or hair.

Wigs were real big in the 1960s, and after the experience my mom had when her hair fell out–like when you see the old black and white TV show episodes of the Lucy Show of the same experience–my mom wore a wig until her hair grew back, and I decided it would be a good idea for me when I go-go danced. There was a beauty store that is still there today in 2015. I went in and looked at all the beautiful styles. My hair was very fine and I always needed shampoos to make my hair look thicker. I had seen a beautiful long haired wig which I thought was called a wig but then was called a Fall that you would attach to your own hair. It matched my own hair color perfectly. It was a human hair fall and I loved it. I did not try it on in the store, I just bought it.

I went home and took bobby pins to put it onto my scalp. I combed my own hair over it and it looked beautiful. My own hair never grew too long like my girlfriend Cleo's or Jackie's. It only stopped growing at the top center of my back. The fall was closer to my waist and looked glamorous with a Hollywood movie star look with the outfit I bought at the Cameo Shop. Now when I danced I wouldn't have to worry about looking like a drowned rat.

I was at the jukebox with my new outfit and fall picking my songs to dance to. A guy came over to me with a dark blue navy three quarter length leather jacket with a belt. He was somewhat handsome, not as handsome as the other guys that I remember in the 1960s. He said "Hi! My name's Nick. What's yours? Can I take you out?" He was so, what you would call in those days, "fast," and I said "Get lost," as I did not fraternize with customers after certain experiences–we were told not to. He was just too fast moving, and I didn't know him. As time went on, this guy Nick was persistent and kept coming up to me on different nights to ask me to go out on a date, and I just plainly said, "No."

There was a barmaid named Desiree who bartended and lived upstairs above Joey's Lounge. As time went on Desiree must have heard Nick repeatedly asking me to go on a date with him, and me saying, "No," to him, because I didn't know him. Desiree said to me as I was at the bar, "Fay, Nicky's okay! I grew up with him." Fay was my nickname I always used growing up. I didn't answer and said nothing. My favorite boy's name was always Nicky, but I didn't think anything of it at the time this guy Nick came to ask me for a date. One night Nick came again to ask me out and I said, "Yes, okay," because Desiree approved of him and knew him.

He asked me to go out on Mother's Day in May of 1970. The first night I met him was in April of 1970, so it was a month later I accepted his date because of Desiree, the barmaid, who made me feel more comfortable since she grew up with him. I told Nick, "I'll go out with you, but I have another date that night, and it's Mother's Day, and I have to be home by 5 PM." He said "I'll bring you home by five," and I accepted and gave him my address.

On Mother's Day in May of 1970, my mom may have been sleeping and I didn't wake her up. I got dressed to go out with Nick. It was a beautiful warm spring day, that day with sunshine. I think if I can remember he showed me his car one night. It was dark, almost navy blue, a small Volkswagen car. And I could remember saying, "A big guy like you in a little car like this?" I was used to seeing the big luxury Cadillacs the guys drove in, which was always my favorite style of car, although I personally never drove a car. So Nick picked me up, and we were out on our first date together. He said we'd go out to East River Drive here in Philadelphia.

We stopped at a 7-Eleven store to buy soda. In those days, in 1970, here in Philadelphia, there was no plastic soda bottles that you could just twist off. There were only glass soda bottles with a metal cap and you needed a can opener, which was a small tool. So Nick went into the 7-Eleven and bought two six packs of Pepsi Cola and a can opener. He asked me if I wanted a soda, and I said, "Yes." As we were driving, I opened one for him and me with the can opener. By mistake, when I gave him the soda, he drank that one and wanted another and opened it himself. He mistakenly threw out the can opener instead of the Pepsi Cola soda cap. And we were stuck with two six packs of soda and no can opener to open the remaining soda packs. When we got to East River Drive, Nick parked his Volkswagen close to a tree. We sat by the tree to talk and to get to know each other. He told me about his baby brother and showed me a picture of him. He was a cute little boy with glasses, and he looked like he was in second grade. It was Mother's Day but we didn't really talk about our moms. He asked me if I was going to do anything with my mom this day, and I said, "Not really, but I'll see her when I get home." My mom and I never really celebrated Mother's day. It really wasn't important to my mom and I don't think she even knew it was Mother's Day that day. Nick and

I stayed for about an hour by the tree and it was nice. We also drove around in his Volkswagen, and he had an interest in a new type of music in those days when the Beatles became popular. He had music like the Doors, Moody Blues, which really did not interest me at all at that time, but our time together that day was a nice day.

I reminded him I had a date for the night and Nick brought me home by 5 o'clock that night. My mom was somewhere in the house, probably doing cleaning. I tidied myself up and went out with an Italian guy named Vincent, who I knew before I met Nick. I was on two dates that Mother's Day in 1970. Then I came home to sleep. I now remember that I wished my mom a Happy Mother's Day before I went out with Nick at 12 PM noontime, when Nick picked me up at our home in Philadelphia PA at the address of 2718 East Madison St. That was and is a very famous address here in Philadelphia, PA, and no one can buy that house today. And that was my and my family's home.

I was still dancing at Joey's Lounge and happy. Baby Jane and I go along so well and the club was doing great. When I was tired and the club wasn't too busy there was a long bench in the pool room, and I would take a short nap on the bench when no one was playing pool in there. I would just rest without totally falling asleep. Then I would get up after my break and dance again after when Baby Jane was done dancing or any of the other go-go girls or guys.

One night I was on break and sitting at the bar. A big handsome man with a medium colored beige trench coat came into Joey's Lounge. The club was pretty filled with people and I looked at this man. He said directly to me, "Shut the record player off!" I don't know why I said it but I said "I'm not gonna shut that record player off." It was not my place to do that. And this man went behind the jukebox and pulled the plug out of the socket. People were all in there and this was a surprise to me. I did not know why this man was here or who he was or why he was doing this. All of sudden the police came in, and the man in the trench coat said all of the people who were customers or patrons that night have to leave. And they were let out. The man in the trench coat said all of the employees are being arrested. He told me I was being arrested along with the other dancers and employees for soliciting drinks. I told him I didn't solicit no one for drinks because we didn't have to. We got our own drinks, and I always only drank two drinks then and never got drunk. They were orange juice with very little liquor in it. I did not like that this was going on, so I went into that pool room and seen steps that led to a basement and went down there. After a while it was quiet and I figured I'll just stay here and see what happens. The man in the trench coat searched the rest of the club and saw me and said, "Come on." I went with him out the door and here is was about 2 AM, the normal time that clubs closed. We all went into the patrol wagon, which was also known as "paddy wagons," and they were a brighter red on the outside in those days in Philadelphia. Today in Philadelphia, they are white.

So we all were arrested including my boss Joey, and for no good reason that I know of. The police took us to 8th and Race streets. Baby Jane and I were handcuffed together and she's pulling one way and I'm pulling the other way. We were in a small type of jail and drank water from small iron cups. The whole day passed and we were led to a judge to talk to. We were filthy dirty because of the filthy dirty environment. We were able to leave because we did not do anything wrong. I went home, never said anything or thought about that night again.

I went to work still dancing at Joey's Lounge. We had really nice times there. Nick and I were dating, and he was a perfect gentleman. After two weeks of dating he asked me to marry him and I said, "Are you crazy? You don't even know me!" I thought to myself, how can you be in love and want to get married in only two weeks of dating someone? As I think about this in my adult years, he did not waste any time like when he approached me at the jukebox. I said, "Are you serious?" and Nick said, "Yes." We had a lot in common from the two weeks of dating. I don't know how it came about, but it had to be about the songs I was playing on the jukebox that we had the same interest.

There was a song that I never heard of before by Smokey Robinson and the Miracles called "You know that I'm Swept for You Baby." Nick played that song, and then would go into the pool room to play pool. It was a beautiful song and he would sing to it. Nick was four-and-one-half years older than me but we started to have a lot in common. It came about that when I told him a little about myself of having gone to Frankford High school here in Philadelphia, I asked if he knew anyone from there and I started mentioning a lot of my friends. Here we both knew the same people at one time or another, maybe at the same places we had gone to, but we never met then. I never knew him, never seen him and he never seen or knew me. All of the friends I talked about were older than me like Nick, but there was also friends my age and we all paled around together.

It's hard when you are growing up to always be with people exactly the same age. It's as if you are with your sisters and brothers, and how can you all be the exact same age unless you are twins, triplets, quadruplets, etc.? It's impossible. So Nick was four-and-one-half years older, coincidentally, like the boyfriend Joe I had dated for five years, whose dad made the famous Sally Starr's boots.

I loved the name Nicky and that was a coincidence also and I always called him Nicky when I was younger. I brought him home to my house. I had a Pekinese dog then, named Dawn Dawn. Her formal name was Golden Dawn, because she was given to me and my family and born at that time in the morning. When Nicky and I came into my house, I had to go to the bathroom and Nicky sat down on our beautiful John Wanamaker's medium olive green modern looking couch. Nicky didn't know Dawn Dawn was sleeping on the couch, and she was snoring because Pekinese dogs have smaller pushed in noses. After I came downstairs he said to me, "I thought there was another man sleeping here," because Dawn Dawn really snored loud, but Nicky didn't see her and didn't know where the snoring was coming from. I think he felt a little uncomfortable until I told him. I laugh about it today in my adult years.

I introduced Nicky to my mom, Fay. She looked beautiful, as always in her adult years. She had on, as I clearly remember, a black straight dress with a thin belt and it was very becoming on her, the same type of dresses you see in the old black and white movies of the 1940s and 1950s. The three of us talked for a while, then Nicky left to go home. I told my mom after Nicky left that I was going to get married. My mom was surprised and said, "I don't know this man!" It was a little too soon for my mom, at that time, to accept it, as most couples date for a longer time and we only dated for two weeks when I introduced her to him for the first time. My mom was quiet about it and so was I and we left it at that in our conversation.

Nicky wanted me to meet his parents and I told him I'll take a taxi cab and he gave me the address. It was early evening before dark in May. I had bought a beautiful pale yellow empire dress with white felt daisies on it at a store called the Sample Hut in Bala Cynwyd, PA. I had a light hot pink, sort of floppy hat, from when I danced on the Hy Lit TV show that I wore that night to meet Nicky's parents. Nicky's home was a big twin home and was located at 4427 N. 8th St. here in Philadelphia, PA, close to Hunting Park Ave and the Boulevard. I came in from the taxi cab, and Nicky introduced me to his mom. She had curlers in her hair. I don't think she knew, like my mom, that we were going to tell her we were getting married. His dad was not there yet, but came shortly with a newspaper in his hand and sat down on a chair. He introduced me to his dad and Nicky told his parents he wanted to marry me. His parents, like my mom, were quiet about it and it was a nice get-together and start of preparing for a wedding.

I was still dancing at Joey's Lounge and was so happy. Nicky was there at the club every night. Before my having met Nicky I was thinking of making a choice with my career. I was either going to go to New York City, NY to join the dance group the Rockettes, or go to school to become a hairdresser. But when I met Nicky we fell in love and he said "I'm going to take you away from all this." Nicky did not want to me go-go dance or dance at all, as I was going to be his wife, and I was happy.

Photographers took pictures of the dancers and we had 8x10 black and white glossy pictures on the walls at Joey's Lounge. I told everyone that I danced with that I was getting married to Nicky, and they were happy for me. On my last night of dancing at Joey's Lounge, I chose a song at the jukebox by the Supremes to dance to for my last night. It was called "Someday We'll Be Together," and I received a lot of cheers. Nicky was so happy and so were his parents, that we were getting married.

Now I had to plan our wedding with our families. Nicky wanted for us to have an engagement party at his home. He told his parents and they planned it. I told all of my friends and invited them. My mom and uncle Frankie, as time went on, really liked him and it was a son my mother never had, as I was her only child. I helped, on my own, without saying anything to anyone and went to some party store or a five-and-dime store and found a beautiful large Lucite engagement ring to put on top of the cake. It had light gold glitter on the inside of the Lucite stone, and if you would shake it the glitter would dance inside the stone, like the Christmas glitter balls you see at Christmas time.

Nicky wanted me to meet the rest of his family as we were making wedding plans, and he said "The only thing I have to offer you is my family." Now, in my adult years I realize what he said to me, because it went so fast, just like a wedding day goes fast, even if it's a long day, or even if your life seems long, it goes by fast and you'll miss it.

So Nicky and I went over to his dad's youngest sister's house. Her name was Carmella. Nicky introduced me to her as she was putting a vacuum cleaner away in the closet. She was married, but her husband, whose name was Dick, was working. He worked for the Budd Circuit Company on Grant Ave here in Philadelphia, PA, where they made circuit boards. I think they may have even made them for TVs, I'm not sure. As time went on, tragedy struck with Carmella's husband and he died from acute leukemia at the young age of thirty-two-years-old. He left her with four small children to raise and later tragedy struck for her again and again in later years. Her real name was Nicole. But before all this tragedy everyone in Nicky's family and my family had a lot of happy times that I'll never forget.

The night of my engagement came and I wore a beautiful, what you would call a Tablecloth dress. I had an older girlfriend who lived in my neighborhood in Port Richmond by the name of Violet, whom I babysat for occasionally, and before I even met Nicky, she gave me this dress. It was from another famous women's fashion store called Irene Lee's in Kensington, which is next to Port Richmond, where me and my mom shopped at other stores. It was light ivory colored with a large baby blue bow in the back and had thin 1" straps and was A-lined shaped, and A-line dresses were big fashion in the 1960s. It was right below the knee and fit me perfectly, even though Violet was much smaller than me. I wore this dress on my engagement party night with silk silver shoes that had a Queen Anne heel that I bought from Baker's Shoe Store in downtown Philadelphia. These shoes I also go-go danced in. They were ladylike with a little bow on top. I had my hair done for my engagement party in French Curls and the hairdo was called the Gibson Girl. I wore sheer nylon stockings to match my skin.

Nicky's cousin, Kate, made my engagement cake and brought it downstairs to the basement. I put the Lucite glitter ring on top and made a heart out of paper and wrote "Nicky & Fay" on it, and taped it above the cake on a paneled wall. All my friends and Nicky's family were coming. My mom and Uncle Frankie met Nicky's dad and mom for the first time. All my dance friends and my boss Joey from Joey's Lounge came. Violet, who gave me the beautiful tablecloth dress, came with my older girlfriend Janice, who lived in my neighborhood and was Violet's real close friend. Other friends of mine came too. The house was fully packed and I didn't know any of Nicky's other relatives yet, as I had only met his aunt Carmella. There was plenty of food, but I wasn't hungry and did not eat that night. I was downstairs in the basement, and Nicky's family started coming downstairs too with my friends and gifts. Nicky came downstairs, and I could remember he wanted to give me my engagement ring before our engagement party, which was weeks before the engagement party. He asked me what kind of ring I wanted and I did not want the common, usual type of engagement ring that is considered traditional as most girls get for their engagement. I loved daisies at that time and I told him, "I want a cocktail ring that looks like a daisy."

On the night of my engagement party before all our guests arrived, he wanted to give it to me before they came. I said wait until everyone gets here to show me as I wanted to be surprised and our friends and family to also see it for the first time. We were downstairs in the basement and others were upstairs. Nicky opened the box and gave me the engagement ring. It was beautiful and looked like a different kind of daisy flower. It had two rows of swirled petals with a one carat round diamond in the center. The total ring size was two-and-one-half carats and the size of almost a nickel, five cent coin, and set in white platinum gold as I wanted it all one color to match the diamonds and the silver color of white platinum gold blended. I thought in my mind at that time in 1970 a silver color with the diamonds. It was a beautiful ring, and I showed it off to everyone at our engagement party who wanted to see it. Nicky and I kissed, and someone took pictures of us and my engagement ring. Later, as time went by, Nicky told me that a neighbor, who lived across the street and who was close friends of Nicky's parents, by the name of Ken Gilman, was a jeweler and custom-made my engagement ring. Ken Gilman and his wife, Diane, came to our engagement party. It was a happy time.

The next day I went to Nicky's house, and his mom and I stayed together as I opened our engagement gifts. I got very expensive gifts. I remember getting an ornate silver tray with a silver sugar and creamer set that was a gift from the Gilmans. There were so many gifts I can't remember who they all came from now. Nicky had a cousin named Trixie, and her real name was also Nicole. Trixie had a younger sister named Christy who in later years became my favorite cousin on Nicky's dad's side, but she never knew it. I can remember getting an electric toaster oven and I loved it and used it all the time and only made sirloin steaks on it. This is the one gift I remember from Nicky's cousins Trixie and Christy. Another gift was from Nicky's aunt and uncle, named David and Doris Emmett, on Nicky's side of the family. It was an electric carving knife. I used it all the time for Easter, Thanksgiving, and Christmas holidays, and it was a great modern invention and a lot easier in later years.

I remember receiving a beautiful white satin bag, what the higher class of people called a "money bag," for placing envelopes of money gifts at weddings. This gift was from a close friend of my parent's named Daniel and Patricia Smith. Mrs. Smith told me the white satin money bag can also be converted into a baby's pillow case. It was plain, with white lace around the edges and satin piped handles for carrying the bag. My friend, whose name was also Christy, like Nicky's cousin, could not come to our engagement party. Christy and I grew up together from the age of eleven, and I wanted her to be in my wedding. I was supposed to have, for which I chose at that time, about or close to thirteen bridesmaids. The close friends I chose, either I could not reach or they could not be in my wedding because of problems they may have had. I do not know. But I was happy, the two twin sisters Erica and Joyce Mainer, that were truly and really my best friends and sisters to me from the time we were about six-years-old after Vivian became my closer and truer friends even until this day in 2015. The three of us are coincidentally the same age.

I was really close to Erica. Joyce was about one minute older than Erica about from the twin birth. They were beautiful girls growing up with dark brown/black hair. People used to say to me, "How can you tell them apart?" I would always say Erica has smaller, slant-y oriental eyes, and Joyce has bigger round eyes. When Nicky and I were planning our wedding without our families, I wanted Erica to be my maid of honor, but Erica was married. I wanted to get married at Nicky's parish, St. Henry's Catholic Church, because my parish, St. George's, had a lot of steps to walk up before you got into the church and it was too small for all the guests that would be invited. So I got permission from my Catholic Church, St. George's, to be married at St Henry's, Nicky's parish. St. Henry's pastor told me that since Erica is already married, she could be my matron of honor. I was close to Joyce also, but not as close to Erica, and I didn't want to hurt Joyce. The pastor told me, Joyce can be your maid of honor and Erica will walk down the church aisle first, after you, then Joyce. So it was planned perfectly, with my twin sister girlfriends.

Now I had a problem not being able to get the rest of the girlfriends I wanted to be in our wedding and talked about it with Nicky. He said, for which I had already met them and they lived also across the street from Nicky's parents, "How about asking my cousin Kate and her younger sister Anna?" I was not really fully satisfied with asking them to be in our wedding because I didn't have no relationship with them. I really didn't know them, and it was taking away sentimental value of my friends that I grew up with. But I had no other alternative. Since they were Nicky's cousins it would be acceptable to me. I asked Agnes and Anna, they discussed it with their parents and they were happy, really happy to be chosen to be in our upcoming wedding.

My tap dancing teacher's daughter, Ann, –Karen's first child–was old enough to be in our wedding but too old to be a flower girl and too young to be a bridesmaid. I didn't know what to do for this situation either. Stan Jr., my favorite of my tap dancing teacher's children, was still a baby and too young to be in our wedding. The pastor told me Ann could be the junior bridesmaid. At least I had Erica, Joyce, and Ann that would have sentimental value to me. So they were the only three, in my childhood days of growing up and who I was close to that would be in our upcoming wedding. For a flower girl, Nicky had a cousin on his mom's side that we chose. Her name was Marsha Adler, Nicky's mom's last maiden name.

The ring bearer was Nicky's aunt Carmella's youngest boy. Later in years, when he was about the age of thirty, he committed suicide for reasons I do not know. This was another tragedy for Nicky's aunt Carmella. Her first son, Dick, like her husband Dick, also died of Leukemia when he was in about his forties. Nicky's aunt Carmella has one daughter left also named Carmella, and one son Carl from her first marriage to Dick. After his death and raising her children, she married a divorced man ten years younger than her and she was not happy because she loved her first husband Dick. To me it was all a phony facade, putting on airs and she was untrue to herself, from all of her brother's poor advice, which were about to become my uncles through marriage to Nicky. My grandfather, Charles Embris, once told me, "Italians are liars," and I truly believe this with certain experiences I had as time went on. And I truly believe when you constantly tell lies you are lying to yourself.

So the people who were chosen so far for our wedding were Erica, Joyce Mary, Anna, Lisa, and Bobby–real name was Robert. I chose Erica's husband Franny, real name: Francis Stycenski, to be bridegroom as I grew up with Erica and Franny. Also Erica and Franny met as teenagers and later married when he came home from serving in the Vietnam War in the 1960s. I chose Joyce's husband Andrew Lebski, who also served the Vietnam War, and Joyce and Erica both met Franny and Andrew as teenagers at the same time. The twin sisters married two best friends. Andrew came home safe and was well after him, and Joyce married but in later years developed paralysis and diabetes. He passed away several years ago and served the front lines of the Marine Corps. Franny also was a Marine, but did not serve the front action lines. He and Erica are happy together today.

Nicky now had to choose the remaining bridegrooms for our wedding. He chose his Uncle Carl and uncle Eddie, which when I think of it today they were kind of old. Why didn't he choose the friends he grew up with? But I didn't say anything. It was his choice. He also chose his cousins Anthony Adler and Michael Adler who were brothers. His Uncle Vincent and Uncle Eddie were half-brothers and last name also was Adler, and another Michael Adler who was bridegroom and now deceased, married to Constance, on Nicky's mother's side. He chose another cousin named Eddie, who was Mary's younger brother, and he was a bridegroom with Anna, his sister. Nicky's brother, Peter, after Nicky's dad, was junior bridegroom and walked with Ann, my tap dancing teacher's first child, down St. Henry's church aisle.

Before the wedding I found temporary jobs such as typing medical reports at Northeastern Hospital in Philadelphia, PA, in my neighborhood in Port Richmond, and it was located on Allegheny Ave and Cedar St., or close to Cedar St., and worked typing these reports for a Doctor Tenet. It was fun and comfortable because Vivian was there. Vivian's ex-husband was a sketch artist for the police department and highly regarded. You would never expect Vivian and her husband to be a couple. Vivian was like a Lucille Ball, and Mr. Lang was more serious, naturally, because of his profession. But they remained close, even after divorcing, because of their two daughters, Donna and Linda, whom I used to babysit for in the 1960s. We were the happiest in our neighborhood of Port Richmond, in Philadelphia PA. No one could take that away from any of us, who lived there, not anyone.

I had to find and buy my wedding gown. Since I worked for the JC Penney credit offices and company, I wanted to buy my wedding gown from there. They had beautiful gowns and the highest clientele in sales. I talked about it with Nicky and he said his cousin Adam can have my wedding gown made. My wedding gown and veil and flowered crown were custom-made at a bridal sewing corporation Adam worked at. I chose to go to the famous bridal salon store in downtown Philadelphia, PA called Silverman's for the bridal party. They had chiffon and velvet empire gowns that matched my style of bridal gown as the empire style was big in the 1960s to when I would marry in 1970. Erica, my matron of honor, wanted me to wear the fuller type of bridal gown, but that style was just not "in vogue" then and I would not have felt in vogue and chose the umpire, A-line style. Today, anything goes; it is your wedding and fun to plan if your plans work out and you have to oversee everything to make sure it goes right. Remember though, nothing and no one is perfect, but should be trusted when it involves you and your wedding, especially with a lot of disasters that were reported and unreported.

I worked at Northeastern Hospital alongside a girl my age named Julia Mauratis and told her I was getting married and we were planning for our wedding and I needed a hall with catering. Erica and Joyce wanted me to have our wedding at the hall my grandfather Stephen built. I don't know why, I just did not want to have it there. Maybe I wanted a change of atmosphere at that time. I first chose a beautiful catered hall called the L & M Caterers, but there was a two-year waiting list for evening nighttime receptions and only the daytime was available. In the Roman Catholic religion then, you married in church in the morning and your reception was in the evening when the sun went down and you celebrated all day in between at families' homes until leaving for the evening reception, and I would not have it any other way.

So Julia Mauratis told me about a catered hall in South Philadelphia called the Candlelight Caterers. I believe it was on Oregon Ave then, and Nicky's family was Italian and it would be good. I told Nicky, and we went to see it and it was beautiful. When you walked in there were large black and white checkered floors and a medium sized raised stage for dancing that had a beautiful pale ivory French provincial wrought iron railing surrounding the stage. The lady who was the owner, caterer as well as coordinator for the Candlelight Caterers was very nice. She planned everything for us and told us that if we didn't have an outside source for music, they had musicians. I was happy with this and chose her recommendation to stay with their music. Nicky was happy with this also. We told our bridal party and the plans were made. The lady at the Candlelight Caterers told me the open date she had was for Saturday, November 7, 1970, right before my birthday, November 26th, on Thanksgiving Day. Nicky and I and our families were so happy.

I got my hair styled in a famous hairdo that I wanted called the Gibson Girl. It was hair all pulled up with loose curls on top and a few loose curls at the sides of the temples and at the sides of the ears. When I see brides today with hanging, straight hair or un-classic, that they call classic today, I think to myself, look how ugly they are. They have no etiquette or style at all. Why even be a bride? Weddings are supposed to be beautiful, especially the bride. They do need to go to etiquette and charm school. Even though I never went to etiquette or charm school, I had some sense when I was to marry of how to look just by looking at past bridal books that retained the classic elegance. And professional people in the wedding business as well as my family guided me the right way.

When Nicky and I planned our wedding, there was not any arguments. Our wedding was not exactly perfect, but it still was beautiful and everyone worked hard and did the best they could. I noticed when we received our wedding album and I didn't notice it at the hall when the pictures were taken that the drapes either shrunk or they could not get long enough drapes or someone misjudged making them and they were too short and did not reach the floor. It was a picture of me, Anna, and Ann with them leaning on my two shoulders on each side. It was a beautiful picture, except for the drapes, and I laugh about it today and you will to at your wedding, if you get married, when things like this happen.

My beautiful mom, now aged, was so happy and proud. She was a big movie star in her day. She got married on Valentine's Day in Atlantic City and it remains a mystery of what happened as there are no more photos left or books to prove it. Everything is falsified, even the divorce papers of having been married to Army Lieutenant John Alex Wills, for whom I never saw or known. I only remember the dads who took care of me, which no one would believe, or care to believe, and only would want to get close to me because of Al Laurentis, whom I believe married my mom Anne in Atlantic City on Valentine's Day. As on my Communion day, the five gentlemen that were at my Aunt Jean's for my communion, and I remember were Al Laurentis, his brother Jimmy, another man who was related to Al Laurentis named Jimmy, and Anthony and Stephen, all with the same last name of Laurentis, except I know Stephen did not have that last name.

The books you see in the stores show a woman named May who says was his wife and mother of Alberto Laurentis. I don't know but I can remember and seeing my mom crying and calling Joe, who was maybe Al's brother or cousin, but I never seen or knew a John Alex Wills, a lieutenant for the United States Army. I only seen these five men who took care of me and later like I said in previous pages of when I was go-go dancing, before I met Nicky, that Al's brother Joe brought me home one night from the Gaslight West, because the Red Arrow bus lines stopped running and I could not get a taxi that night in the 1960s and he was kind enough to offer me a ride and drive me home and I remember that clearly today in my adult years.

He lived in Port Richmond in Philadelphia, PA, in my neighborhood. He also was in the US Army and he was tough like his brother Al. When I used to go to Josie's Candy Store, diagonally across the street from my house located at Salmon and Madison streets, and is now made into a home with the storefront, he would come into the store and buy soda for which you handpicked from a large refrigerator steel box, and then paid Josie or Mike Ciosek. This was when I was a young girl from seven-years-old and up to my teen years, before I became a go-go dancer.

After not ever seeing who was supposedly my real father, John Alex Wills, as written on my birth certificate and so hard to believe because only the five men that I told you about were at my communion party. They were Al Laurentis, his brother Joe, his brother Anthony, and another relative named Joe and a Michael. Today people would find it hard to believe this, and I never talked about it to anyone. I never knew, until my adult life, as I look back: there was nothing to brag about, as my Uncle Frankie would say. So, that is some of my childhood and teenage life.

Nicky and I were young and happy. Only I didn't know how hard it would be, after we got married and all the glitz and glamour of a beautiful wedding wore off after our wedding day.

Nicky wanted to have his own family and as I said, as fast as he was, wanted a baby right away. He didn't care if it was a boy or girl as long as she or he was healthy. I was now in waiting as the old saying goes, and my gynecologist said that I was pregnant. Nicky was happy and so were his parents and my mom and Uncle Frankie. I would hold my stomach in and did not show it until eight months of being pregnant at my baby shower. I was given two baby showers. The first from my tap dancing teacher, Karen, and her husband's aunts—Ellen, Dorothy and Angie–the sisters that I told you about who were Stan's mom Kathleen's sisters and who was killed by his dad from acid spilled in her face so one would ever look at her beauty ever again. My second baby shower was from my mother-in-law, Marie, nicknamed Patty. I received loads of baby shower gifts and had enough for maybe three years of not having to buy too much!

I remember getting a beautiful shiny light, silver, stainless steel piggy bank from the Gilmanss. I got a fancy silk silver iridescent baby photograph book from my favorite cousin on Nicky's side, Christine, and her older sister Trixie. And lots of homemade crocheted baby clothes, as well as store bought baby clothes, etc.

Nicky and I were invited, after the baby shower, to my older girlfriend Violet's house along with my older girlfriend Janice. I was eight months pregnant and had on navy blue corduroy maternity pants with a red, white and blue horizontal striped maternity cotton blouse that my tap dancing teacher, Karen, had given me from when she was pregnant and it fit even though she was small and shorter than me. I did not want to spend or waste money on fancy maternity clothes that only were worn for nine months. I had maybe about six tops total. I bought a Mickey Mouse short sleeved t-shirt and a dressier ivory peasant like knit blouse and Karen gave me two more maternity tops and I bought only two pairs of corduroy pants from Sears and Roebuck catalogue. That was it for nine months of carrying my child.

Well, to get back to being at Violet's for an evening get together. Violet was pouring coffee in all of our cups. When she came to pour my coffee, the hot coffee cup spilled onto my corduroy pants and stuck to my skin. It was hot black coffee, an accident, but Nicky and I had to leave. Nicky said, "Do you want to go to the hospital," and I said, "No, let's go home, unless I really need to later." When I got home I tried to take my corduroy pants off, but they were sticking to my thigh leg skin. I slowly pulled them off and I really had painful layers of skin come off onto my pants. I quickly got ice wrapped in a wet cold towel and put it on my thigh to ease the burning. I stayed up all night to care of this. Nicky stayed with me, but he really didn't know what to do and was very quiet, and I think, a little alarmed without showing it as strong as he was. I was able to finally rest and get some sleep with the cold wet towel on my right thigh.

The next day I couldn't walk very well and my skin was burned and I had to walk with a limp because it burned so bad. I was thankful the hot black coffee didn't fall on my stomach. What would have happened if it did, with carrying my child and being eight months pregnant? It was scary. I could not wear long pants after that and had to wear real short pants to constantly air the bad burn on my thigh. Into my ninth month of pregnancy, I was able to straighten my leg as the painful burn subsided, but I had a great scar about ten inches in diameter and was a dark brown but disappeared in about four to seven years. I was happy the hot black coffee didn't fall on my stomach. It was an accident and Violet was worried, but I told her it was okay now.

My gynecologist, Dr. Singleton, told me that when my labor pains are a minute apart in my ninth month of pregnancy to phone him so he could plan for my delivery of my child. When that time came, I did not wait until the labor pains were one minute apart. I did not want to wait until that time of being so short of time because I remember hearing of women having babies in cars, etc., because once their water broke, the baby was coming. When my labor pains were five minutes apart, I called Dr. Singleton. He told me to come to the hospital, which was the old Frankford Hospital on Frankford Avenue, close to Bridge and Pratt streets. That hospital is still there today, in addition to a new one build on Academy road in here in Philadelphia PA. Nicky was with me at our apartment and ready to drive me to the hospital in his royal blue Volkswagen. We got in the car, and guess what? The car wouldn't start. It worked from the time I met him and of all times, that night, the car would not start. Nicky said he'll have to call his father. Time was passing and the labor pain was severe. His dad quickly came in about fifteen to twenty minutes. The three of us went to the old Frankford Hospital.

When I got to the hospital, I went through procedures such as being shaved before having the baby which was considered sterile in those days of now the 1970s when I was having my child. There was no such thing as ultrasound as you have today in the 2000s to determine if your child was a boy or girl, for which I would not want anyway. I wanted to be surprised. After being shaved, I had to take an enema to be cleansed of my bowels. The pain was up and down now. I did not have any bowel movement and lifted up my housecoat to look in the bathroom mirror of the first time being shaved, and I laughed because it looked funny.

I went into the labor room and Nicky was with me. I laid down and the pain was coming on. Dr. Singleton had his assistant Dr. Flynn there for me as Dr. Singleton was called for another delivery of a baby since my delay of getting to the hospital because of the car not starting. Dr. Flynn ordered to have me induced, which is to bring on forced labor as I was near delivery but still not ready.

I was at the Old Frankford Hospital now for three days. I was given intravenous to force the labor and it was excruciating pain. It was so bad on my back for which my tap dancing teacher, Karen, told me about the lower back pain I would have, that I got out of bed with the needles in my arm to want to rest my back against the wall. A short time later, a nurse came in and said, "You'll never have the baby if you sit up, you have to lay down." I laid down and suddenly my favorite singing group, the Temptations, came to mind. It was strange, as if I was dreaming, and I told Nicky beside me. Dr. Flynn came into my room, and told Nicky as Nicky was so tired, "You might as well go home, she's not going to have the baby yet, and come back in the morning and get some rest." Nicky kissed me goodbye.

I was waiting and the labor pains were coming closer and stronger. I was beginning to dilate and that gave Dr. Flynn and the nurses the signal I was ready to deliver my child. I was brought into the delivery room. I thought now the baby would be easily taken out, but little did I know I had to work and push like a bowel movement. It was painful. Dr. Flynn said, "Keep on pushing." He signaled me that my child was coming, and my knees were like a vibrating machine from the shock of the pain. Before I knew it I heard him say, "It's all done, you have a baby girl," and he showed me her and put the gas mask on me to be able to sleep after three days. I never experienced excruciating pain like that ever. They say that men experience the pain of wisdom teeth being pulled wanting to know how it feels to have a baby, but it's not even close to that. It's much more painful than wisdom teeth being pulled, and many women died on the delivery table form the pain of childbirth. It's traumatic for the mother and child, and I think that is why the baby cries. If the child is not awake, with a slap on the behind from the doctor after waking them, the child cries. After that morning at 12:51 AM when I had my child, I never would want to experience that again. What an experience!

When I woke up from the anesthesia the nurse was so nice and asked me what I wanted to eat. It was about 2 AM, I said, "Two boiled ham sandwiches," and she got them for me. I was in a semi-private room with another first time mother as me and content that she was there, as we had something in common. The nurses brought out babies in at this late hour for us to really see close up for the first time. We both had girls. My child was sleeping, and she was beautiful as any newborn. I was happy the pain had ended and to enjoy seeing and being with my baby, our baby, Nicky's baby.

Dr. Flynn came in and told me she weighed eight pounds, four ounces at birth. He also told me that I'll experience afterbirth pain when all the afterbirth excretes. for which I did not want to hear. My baby was born April 22, 1971. In those days, in the 1970s, they kept you for seven days to enjoy your baby alone, as well as to rest. Today in the 2000s, there are too many children being born, and there is not enough room to keep you that long, only for complications. And most doctors agree on Cesarean birth as they say it is less traumatic.

Every day, three times a day, we seen our babies and fed them. When the nurse would bring her in for the entire seven days I would never unwrap the blanket like a lot of mothers would. I did not want to disturb her contentment after what she went through too. I was very happy and Nicky came to visit us. Nicky's parents came and so did his grandmother and Aunt Carmella. My baby was born two weeks after Aunt Carmella's first husband, Dick, died, and my father-in-law, her brother, wanted to get her sorrow into something happier as she was really in a lot of grief.

My father-in-law Robert asked me when we were alone, and Nicky and his aunt Carmella were visiting the baby window, "Did you pick a name yet?"

I said, "No," but I had four choices that I like: Athena, Zena, Nicole, and Nicole.

My father-in-law said, and I was surprised, "Nicole? That's my mother's name."

I said "Do you want me to name her Nicole?" and he was so thrilled. Believe me, I did not know that was his mother's name or his sister Carmella's real name as I didn't know Carmella or Trixie. So my father-in-law, Robert, and I named my baby, and it was a precious time for me and him as it was his first grandchild and a total coincidence that I chose the name Nicole. I really wanted to name her Zena. When Nicky and his Aunt Carmella came back from the baby window, I told them her name. Nicky was thrilled she was named after his grandmother, who died long ago. And it put a happy smile and sentimental smile on Nicky's aunt Carmella's face.

The grandmother who visited me in the hospital was Nicky's mother's stepmother, Anna. When she asked me so soon in my hospital room, "When are you going to have the next baby?"

I said "never."

She said, "You'll forget the pain,"

I said, "No, I won't."

What a thing to say so soon to a mother on the next day of having a baby.

Two days passed. I was so happy, but I was getting crying spells and didn't know why. I was happy and the doctor, Dr. Flynn, said it was very common and called it the "afterbirth blues," from when your hormones change and you could still be happy but you're crying and don't know why. Because I was happy and there was no reason for me to cry. It was strange. The morning came after seven days at the Old Frankford Hospital, and I was leaving with the baby, my daughter Nicole. That day when the nurse brought her in for us to go home she was crying a lot. I said to the nurse, "she won't stop crying." I tried everything, and that is the first time, I heard her really crying, because all of the seven days before that she was quiet. The nurse told me that it was because we had to test her blood, from her heel.

Well, here she was in my arms screaming her head off and I couldn't stop her from crying. Nicky came to bring me and our baby home to our apartment. It was a beautiful spring day in May of 1971. Since the car was broke we took a bus home. Nicole stopped crying and was content for the bus ride. Nicky and I were happy. We came home to our apartment that I found and picked out from a newspaper. It was in Frankford, close to the Margaret and Orthodox stop on the El. Nicky at first did not want this apartment. He wanted to rent a big townhouse, but I thought it would be too expensive for us and we were just starting out as a young married couple. He had a very good job as a printer like his dad, but I did not want to plunge into anything too expensive. Nicky agreed with me and we got the apartment when we were engaged and moved in when we got married.

I found a beautiful couch and two chairs on Frankford Ave. here in Philadelphia, PA, for only $300, to start with. The bedroom set I picked out from a furniture catalogue. Nicky's dad had a close friend in the furniture business that he owned. At first, I picked out a beautiful Oriental bedroom set, but in those days in the 1970s it had to be shipped from the Orient and would cost $2,000 just for the shipping. The price was too expensive for my way of thinking. There was a beautiful pure white Mediterranean style bedroom set that I had seen in the furniture book and asked about the price. It was about $1,000. I talked with Nicky about it and he said it was okay and the furniture men delivered it. Everything fit perfectly without my even having to measure. I did it and figured it with my eyes. The bassinet baby bed that I received from my tap dancing teacher Karen was used five times from her five children and given to me for my daughter Nicole. I put it in the parlor. We had a nice sized parlor, and you had to go through a hallway in the apartment house to get to a large bedroom. I loved our new apartment and it only cost ninety-five dollars monthly with all utilities included.

When Nicky and I got to our new apartment with our baby, I got an unpleasant surprise. My mother-in-law was in my parlor. I did not invite her. I felt it was our first time together with our new baby, and I really didn't like it. I didn't say anything as it was her first grandchild, but it made me feel a little uncomfortable. I handed her the baby and let well enough alone. It was a first time experience also, for my mother-in-law, as it was for me when I thought about it in later years. She was happy and content and so was Nicky, who was her first son. Deep down inside, I had wanted a son, but my mom and my mother-in-law were hoping for a girl and the two of them got their wish. Now that I think of it, in later years, I was happy I had a girl because it's hard to be a mother and raise a boy. I had seen it with my mother-in-law as she had two sons, now she had her little grandchild girl for which she wanted.

I learned a lot from my tap dancing teacher Karen, just watching her and taking her advice always. She was a great mom to her own children and a tap dancing teacher mom with me and other close friends I grew up with in Port Richmond. Karen was a second mom to me and I started calling her "Mom." She was fussy with sterilizing baby bottles and the rubber pacifiers we had in those days. We did not have the fancy plastic topped pacifiers with the rubber nipple you can buy today. So as soon as I came home to our apartment from the hospital with Nicky and the baby, after handing the baby to my mother-in-law, I started cleaning the marine blue kitchen floor with Mop and Glow that cleans and waxes at the same time. I started to become a cleaning fanatic from my aunt through marriage on my godfather's side. Her name–and she was Lithuanian too–was Ann Cleeris.

I was now a new mom myself for the first time and had some experience because of babysitting for my tap dancing teacher. Her children were like sisters and brothers to me and we all were very close and we were happy.

Time passed and Nicky and I were raising our child Nicole. I remember on that first day, when we brought her home from Old Frankford Hospital, that I was wearing a pale baby blue cloth rain coat–I bought from a Main Line store in Bala Cynwyd, PA when I was dancing as a go-go girl in the 1960s, with black suede, low Queen Anne heels–and I put my hair in a ponytail, carrying our baby home from the hospital. I looked and dressed then like a famous actress named Eva Marie Saint, only not as thick hair as hers when she was in a famous black and white movie with the famous Marlon Brando called "On the Waterfront," and a true story about hard working men like my Uncle Frankie.

Nicky was working for a small printing company called W.R. Johnston, close to 2nd street in downtown Philadelphia PA. He was doing well and his parents and my mom and Uncle Frankie were so happy and proud. Nicky was a dad for the first time. I did the best I could and if there was a problem I called the family for advice, or my baby's pediatrician, Dr. Deoria, who had an office in Frankford. We had a beautiful christening at our apartment, and I met a nice elderly neighbor next door named Mrs. Carnel, who I became close to and family and Mrs. Carnel came to the christening. I chose Constance and Ned to be Nicole's godparents, who were first cousins of Nicky's. They picked out and bought a plain cotton christening outfit for our child, as it was warmer that month, now June 1971. I got a lot of beautiful christening gifts, and Nicole was christened at a Catholic church named St. Joachims in Frankford, close to the Margaret and Orthodox stop on the El.

As she was growing I would put her in the baby swing, after feeding her a bottle of milk. She would sometimes get ornery with the baby swing and didn't like it. I got, what you would call, a baby seat that a child could jump up and down in and put her in it when she was close to twelve months. I attached it to the woodwork at the top of an archway from the parlor into the kitchen.

The seat was called Jumpin Jack and she loved it. I read everything before I utilized it as this was a new experience for me and as time went on. She was now ready to go into a new baby seat called the walker, which gave babies a start before actually learning to walk. She loved it and roamed all over the kitchen and parlor.

There was a kitchen door that led to the hallway for which I kept closed, because if she went into the hallway it would be dangerous as it was close to rather long steps. Some days I would keep the door open but would watch her and tell her no and bring her away from the kitchen door. When Nicky would come home and see her in the walker she would be happy and excited to see her daddy. As weeks went on, when I would put her in the walker, she really didn't go near the kitchen door. I left the door open and on one day she knew the pattern of hearing him from down stairs opening the front door and coming up the steps. She flew out the kitchen door excitedly and was going near the hallway steps. I quickly ran to her, and she was down two steps and I grabbed the walker as Nicky was walking up the steps. The walker was great, but you had to watch every single second when your child was in it, especially near steps or anything un-level.

We had a 1 year old birthday party for our daughter with relatives and also Mrs. Carnel, my next door neighbor. Before her one year old birthday party, I would hold her hands, from about 10 months, and walk her in front of me like most mothers do when teaching them how to walk. I would try letting her go, but she couldn't walk on her own yet and I would catch her. This day, on her first birthday party, and with relatives there, I was in the parlor talking with some relatives and Nicole was in the kitchen with relatives. All of sudden she came walking into the parlor and was walking back and forth from the parlor into the kitchen. I said, "Look! She's walking for the first time, and it's her first birthday!" I remember seeing Nicky's Uncle Mike, on his mom's side, sitting by the archway in the kitchen. I was happy she was walking on her own and she was, too. It may have been a mere coincidence, but it was a great, happy first birthday party, believe it or not. Nicky's uncle Mike was watching her and I wonder if that helped her to walk that day. Nicky's uncle Mike is the uncle who a Dr. Plasario said, that Nicky is going to be a big boy like his uncle Mike and he was in his adult years later on.

Nicole, now walking, would meet her daddy every night when she heard him coming up the steps and she didn't go near the steps. She would look out from the wooden stair rail. One day, on a weekend day, when Nicky was home from work, she stuck her head in between the wooden stair rails and I could not get her head out. It's unbelievable how she got her head in, but I couldn't get her head out. I was getting a little worried and called Nicky, who was in the parlor. He came and tried to get her head out, and she wasn't actually crying, but she was starting to fuss and ready to. Nicky slowly wiggled her head from side to side and got her free. It was quite another experience for us as new parents.

The diapers were never ending, changing them every half hour so she wouldn't get diaper rash. My tap dancing teacher taught me to put Desitin on with Johnson's Baby Powder on top. It really prevented diaper rash as Desitin was a medicated cream, and it worked better than just baby powder alone. I laugh about it today in my adult years, but it was really hard.

My mother-in-law, Marie, was starting to become a little possessive with the baby and so was my father-in-law Peter. They came over every single night practically to see the baby and were becoming a nuisance to me. I felt uncomfortable as time passed, as my in-laws were wearing out their welcome, as the old saying goes. But I didn't say anything. Time passed and my mother-in-law was acting extremely rude as years went on. She was very jealous and would talk against a lot of people in the family to get me to agree or side with her. In later years, she was doing it to a first cousin of mine named Bea or Beatrice, and later to my sister-in-law, Michelle. It seemed to be a facade to me as years went on, and I felt they were just putting on facade. That means trying to make yourself look good in front of other people. My in-laws were a nuisance and Nicky told them about and it got a little better. I was an only child and did things on my own before I got married, and just was not used to this, but I didn't say anything until one day to him.

When I was over at my tap dancing teacher's apartment, when she had left her husband Stan because of him having an affair with Karen's brother's wife–who everyone called Sis or Aunt Sissy–I stayed there every weekend with my daughter as Karen and I were very close, and Nicky was working weekends in the printing business. Stan and Karen got back together again after this horrible time that left an effect. Karen was working below at a famous pizza shop called Tiny's, but Tiny was a big Husky man and very good to Karen. Stan and Karen were together again, and everyone was happy. They had a beautiful home at Richmond and Ontario streets. Tiny's pizza restaurant was not too far, at Frankford and Ontario streets.

One day at our apartment, before going to Karen's, I made a tuna fish sandwich for Nicky to bring to work that Saturday. I was in the parlor, and my daughter was playing with their youngest son, Johnny. Nicky was not in the parlor with me, but he was in the hallway at Karen's with Karen's first daughter, who was now grown up. I looked from the parlor and seen the two of them embraced in a lovers kiss, and he handed her the bagged tuna fish sandwich that I made him and left for work. I didn't say anything and did not say anything to Nicky, until twenty-five years after the incident. It surprised me, but I really did not love him truly after that. As years went on, I stayed with him but had no love for him as he was not true. In my adult years, it was like repeated history of something you don't want and didn't want to begin with. I put on a facade just like his parents did. There was no reason for this, only maybe Ann was falling in love with something I had, that she seen in us and wanted. But it left only bitterness amongst everyone for what Nicky did.

Nicky didn't know anything about me before we got married, and I think he just wanted to have an experience of being married and having his own family of something new, beautiful and sacred in his life and his family's life. But it was a shame when this happened and I spoke out and we all drifted apart. I never forgave Nicky for this and just lived with him as a housewife and mother to our daughter. We stayed together for that reason, because of Nicole, but it really wasn't love at all. To me, what I seen in him, he just wanted to have a wedding and then to shame me and everyone else.

When I think about the true story my tap dancing teacher told me, about Stan's mom Kathleen, and later in years I told Nicky about it he said, "Do you call that love?" I thought to myself, "That is the most beautiful love story in the whole world." I wish somebody loved me that much to make me ugly so no one would look at me. And that was a true story. Ann looked like her grandmother Kathleen. She didn't look like my tap dancing teacher, Karen. Ann was beautiful, and I hope that she was happy after that mishap. Nicky in the end was no good, and he turned out to be uglier than I knew.

Nicole was growing up and had a big family on both sides. It was time to move as we just had a one bedroom apartment, and Nicole was in the crib and we slept in a double bed next to the crib. I told Nicky that we had to move because she was getting bigger and needed to have her own bedroom. Nicky agreed, and he wanted something bigger and that felt he was making enough money from his printing job to make a move to something he wanted, which was the new type of modern townhouse. I looked in the newspaper and found a two bedroom townhouse for rent. It was $350 a month plus utilities. I told Nicky and he said, "Let's go see it." It was beautiful and had all the modern kitchen appliances and an outdoor swimming pool for everyone that lived in the townhouse complex. We got beautiful formal French Provincial furniture and sold our first modern furniture set that was in perfect condition for half price through the trade-in times newspaper, which a young couple loved, picked up and bought.

In those days you could trust people; today the younger generation is unskilled and untrustworthy. We moved in and it was a new environment for me. It was not convenient, since I never drove a car, but I made it okay since Nicky drove and we were together to do food shopping on weekends. It was boring and I got into what you would call a housewife's rut, as there really was not anything to do there, except go to the pool in the summer. There was a J.M. Fields store that I found on my own taking Nicole for walks, but it was far and inconvenient for me. Nicky had his big family and I had a lot of friends that I kept in contact with.

I planned a birthday party when Nicole was four years old with a Raggedy Ann and Andy theme, and my mother-in-law Marie made Nicole a Raggedy Ann dress, and I bought her red and white horizontal knee socks and put her hair in what they call pigtails. I planned a game from a party book and made the party game plans myself. Nicky's relatives, younger cousins like my daughter's age of four, and my friends came. Karen came with Ann when Ann was a teenager and her youngest brother Brian. Nicole got a lot of birthday presents and the party was a success.

Time went on and I loved our rented townhouse and made a lot of friends. I found a beauty parlor in the famous Bell telephone book of that time, for which I remember now working for delivering Bell telephone books when Nicky and me had our first apartment in Frankford in Philadelphia, PA. The name of the beauty parlor was the Cosmic Hair Studio. The fad that everyone was into was the singer David Bowie. I really didn't like this music when it came out in the 1970s but my tap dancing teacher's second daughter, Lisa, loved David Bowie and his style. It was a new style for the 1970s and different.

Lisa was a teenager growing up enjoying a new style of music. So, I started listening to it. I loved to try hairstyles, and since it was the 1970s, I wanted to go to the hairdressers to get a hairdo and cut from a professional hairdresser. I told Nicky, and he brought me to the Cosmic Hair Studio. It was the first really modern beauty salon I ever saw, and they had 1970s disco music. I loved the new experience. I didn't know what to ask for in a hairstyle as the hairstyles I wore as a teenager, such as the Pageboy Fluff or French Twist or French curls was not really in style now in the 1970s. We all wore straight hair parted in the middle. So when I sat in the hairdresser's chair, he suggested the David Bowie haircut, and there was a small curl or what they call "spitty" in the front. I loved it. The Cosmic Hair Studio was a new kind of hair salon that styled hair not only for women, but when Nicky seen how good they were, he asked if they cut and styled men's hair and they said, "Yes." When Nicky's hair got a little long and unruly, he made an appointment for the Cosmic Hair Studio. It was a great experience for me with my David Bowie hairstyle. That was my only time there but Nicky liked the way they cut and styled his hair and became a steady customer. The Cosmic Hair Studio still exists.

I was enjoying something new when Nicole was a child called Disco Music. I watched a dance TV show called "Dancing on Air," and watched couples dance. It was something that interested me in that style of music, as well as the dancing, like the teenage days when I watched "Bandstand," "The Ed Hurst Show" in the summer from Atlantic City, NJ, where the Bandstand dancers went in the summer for summer vacation and the Discophonic Scene that a famous disc Jockey named Phil Goldman hosted. I watched "Dancing on Air" every weekend when Nicky was working, but never really talked with him about it.

I still kept in contact and was close with my girlfriend Theresa from Frankford High School. She was dating a guy named Billy and one night I invited them over to our townhouse. Theresa and Billy made a great couple. Nicky and I were happily married and he met my high school girlfriend Theresa and Billy. We talked for a while and Nicky got along well with Billy.

Billy mentioned a new nightclub to go to here in downtown Philadelphia, PA called Harlow's. He said it was a good nightclub and we made plans to meet there the following weekend. I had a lot of beautiful nightclub clothes that I picked out that Nicky bought for me as we went shopping in downtown Philadelphia every weekend and my in-laws babysat out daughter.

The weekend came and Nicky and I were going to the Harlows nightclub. It was located close to 2nd St., where Nicky worked. It was summertime and I bought a black polyester halter dress from the John Wanamaker department store. It looked like a two piece blouse and short skirt, but it was really one piece. The midriff was cut out and the A-line shape of the skirt reached the top of my thighs perfectly as I never wore skirts or dresses shorter than that. The black halter dress was to be worn without showing my naval, although you could adjust it that way, but I did not want my navel to show like most of the trash you see today that are too exposed on the models. There was no label on it and I picked another navy blue, what they call a slip dress, that was A-line shaped with rhinestone spaghetti straps (and I love rhinestones), and right below my knee cap, with a bodice top that looked like a real slip, we always wore slips underneath dresses in the 1960s. Nicky didn't like the black halter dress I chose as much as the navy blue rhinestone spaghetti strap slip dress, but I bought both at the John Wanamaker department store.

The weekend came to go to the Harlow's night club and I wore the black halter dress with low medium red platform leather shoes. There was a line that stretched all the way around the block when we got to Harlow's. It was around the fall, in September, in the 1970s. I bought with Nicky a white leather peplum jacket with an attached white leather belt at Wilson's leather store in downtown Philadelphia, PA, and an off-white men's fedora hat at a store called Daddy Long Legs in Jenkintown, PA. So my outfit for Harlow's was complete. The black halter dress with medium red low platform shoes, my white leather peplum jacket that I wore over my shoulders, my off-white men's fedora hat and white sheer pantyhose stockings.

When Nicky and I got into Harlow's, it was the first time I ever heard or went into a nightclub without a band, that usually in nightclubs in the 1960s sounded terrible and you could not dance to them as they were so off the beat of the music. The first thing I said and I don't know why I said it, was, "Wow, look at this." I didn't know if it was WDAS, but I thought it instantly when I went into Harlow's and kept it to myself. It was a beautiful nightclub with music that had a new sound called stereo and sounded great. It was the first time I ever went to a nightclub that had this quality sound here in downtown Philadelphia, PA.

The Harlow's night club had three levels and a great atmosphere with white small square tables that they call "Parsons Tables," and black and red plastic curtain beads for decoration and atmosphere. It was moderately crowded considering the line of people were around the block waiting to get in. The nightclub was named after the famous movie star Jean Harlow. Nicky and I went there practically every weekend from September to October in the 1970s. We went there one New Year's Eve, and I wanted to get dressed up as the styles turning backwards from the 1940s were in style for nightclubs of the Disco era in the 1970s.

I bought a pair of wide legged, what they called "Bell Bottoms," with small pleats in the front with false cuffs at the bottom of the trouser legs. They were a darker silver and black polyester stretch, with a high waist and side pockets. They called this material Lurex and it shined in dim nightclub lighting. I bought the Lurex bellbottom trousers at a famous store in downtown Philadelphia called Sweet Fanny Adams. I bought a bright red knit vest there also, and I had an idea that would look great for New Year's Eve that year in the 1970s. So I went to the Baum's dance store downtown, where I usually bought trims for dancing as Baum's had everything for entertainers, not necessarily just dancers. I went and bought two feet of bright red Marabou Ostrich feathers to the sleeveless vest and it looked great and overlapped my shoulders slightly. I bought a pair of navy blue suede platform shoes with a three-inch chunky heel at Daddy Long Legs in Jenkintown, PA. They had a cutout toe front with three light turquoise taffeta hearts on the front. These shoes became my favorite shoes that I cherished. I bought a pair of navy blue pantyhose stockings to wear with the shoes.

The outfit looked great and the trousers showed off the shoes perfectly. I set my own hair as it was long then, down the middle of my back, and I wanted to style it in a famous singer's style by the name of Carmen Miranda, who was famous in musicals. I set the front of my hair with curls in bobby pins. I set it in the morning with hairspray, and at night, pulled the rest of my straight hair and bobby pinned it close to the set curls. Then I took the dried hair sprayed curls and combed them loosely and hair-sprayed my entire head. It looked great and would go perfectly with my outfit, for New Year's Eve. Nicky bought platform shoes and bell bottoms, with a tighter shirt and we went to Harlow's. No one was really dancing, as everyone was just having a good time talking and enjoying the music like when you see the old black and white moves of the 1930s or 1940s, or even before that time and they called them "Speakeasy" clubs.

It was great, especially the way we dressed in flamboyance for a nightclub. It really was high class. But one thing I did not know for the Disco era of the 1970s was how to disco dance. I had the style of that time but never learned the dance. Later in years I found out it was called the Hustle. And a famous music artist by the name of Van McCoy composed and recorded an instrumental song called "The Hustle." And in later years, I danced to this song with Nicky, and dancers were doing a famous Polish dance to it called the polka and it turned out perfect.

Harlow's nightclub became a big success and another nightclub of this type opened up in the famous Atlantic City, New Jersey. It was called Rachel's and was a success. Nicky and I really had a great time. We always were together in our younger years when he wasn't working and he stayed close by my side, watched me like a hawk.

We were happy being married, went out every weekend while his family took care of Nicole. I was going to baby showers, wedding showers, and home demonstrations to buy things like Tupperware, home decor, etc. Nicole did not like the separation from me and like most children do but she was safe with my father-in-law Peter and mother-in-law Marie; Nicole was content as time went on, and I felt safe.

The townhouse was getting way too expensive. It was located at 450 Byberry Rd., in Philadelphia PA, and called the "Audubon Estates" in a section called Philmont. They were raising the rent too much as we were putting big money into the townhouse, with expensive wall paper, drapes, paint, etc. It was owned by Sloan Realty and they did not do anything to make it better, only worse, and we were not going to feed them financially. It was an old married couple by the names of Mr. and Mrs. Sloan, and they were eating up everyone's hard work and pay. They were too old to even live in this complex and were making a lot of enemies. It was just getting too expensive too quickly, with extreme raising of the rent, and unfair. We were content there at Audubon

Estates, but they were really getting greedy and money hungry. We had to leave Audubon Estates on Philmont and Byberry Rds., and we, and others, were very unhappy.

Nicky's dad and mom lived in the Hunting Park section in Philadelphia, PA, at the vicinity of 9th and Hunting Park Aves, within walking distance from the Boulevard. There was a vacant house diagonally across the street from Nicky's parents' house and was also a big twin home like theirs. We went to see it. It was very old fashioned on the outside and the inside, except for the kitchen that was more modern looking with a stainless steel sink and modern windows that were small in size and opened up in a new modern way of that time in the 1970s with a handle crank. I was happy because not only did my mother and father-in-law live there, but her sister and my father-in-law's brother lived exactly across the street from them and they were married. He was my Uncle Eddie Mansfield, and she, my Aunt Julia, through marriage. Nicky and I and Nicole moved in our big twin house and being young it was fun for me as I loved being a housewife and mother.

We got settled in, but it took a really long time to unpack and it took months. But I just slowly took my time, enjoying the move, and I had a new family and Nicole and Nicky's family were happy. I had Nicky's first cousin, Karen, who was in our wedding and she got married soon after me. Her husband was named Leo, and they had an old fashioned wedding like Nicky and I. Kate was the first child and daughter of Nicky's Uncle Eddie and Aunt Julia, and Kate, along with her sister Anna and two brothers Eddie and Carl, lived at Nicky's aunt and uncle's house. When Kate and Leo got married, they lived two or three houses away from Nicky and me, with Leo's parents. Kate and Leo grew up together and were childhood boyfriend and girlfriend and then got married. We were all close, and Kate and Joe had their first baby boy, named him Leo. Then later they had another son and named him Cameron. As Nicole was growing up she became close to her cousin Leo, and they played together as Nicole was getting into what they called a "tomboy," playing and having fun with the boys.

Later in years, it was sad as I heard Kate and Leo divorced. Kate was very religious and I could not believe this happened. In the Roman Catholic religion it was "'til death do you part," and I vowed never to get divorced, for the sake of our family and the way I felt. I truly believed these sacred vows, "to love and honor," and "in sickness and in health." As my husband died, in my senior years, I tried to think of the good times and forget about the bad times that all families may have or experience.

Mary's little sister, Anna, got married and it was the first, after Nicky and me got married, that her husband was Lithuanian. I was the first to come into Nicky's large Italian family, as in the early days everyone married their own nationality. Italians married Italians, Polish people married Polish, etc. I was so proud and happy. Anna's husband's name was also Charles, like my father-in-law. We then became very close as Kate and Anna were bridesmaid and junior bridesmaid in my wedding. Anna and Peter lived exactly across the street from me and Nicky. Everyone called Anna's husband "Inky," his nickname.

I now felt comfortable and happy as we all lived on the same block and it was home to me after Nicky and me got married, like it was where I grew up in Port Richmond, a section in Philadelphia, PA, where we all lived in the same neighborhood and were all close. My mom, my real mom, named Fay, and Uncle Frankie were really happy as they were very much welcomed and we all had a lot of parties together and were one huge family. No one was not ever welcomed. We shared the good times as well as the bad times but always stayed together. Even if there was a sad event such as a divorce or a death, we all were close in heart, because in my mind we were family "'til death do you part."

Later, as time passed, Mary's brother, Eddie, who was in my wedding, found a girlfriend. I remember being at my in-laws' house. It was winter time and during the Christmas Holiday on Christmas Eve. Eddie, also known as Little Edie, now was coming in the house that night with a girl. She was a beautiful girl that had a lot of 1970s disco style to her appearance when I look back now. She was smiling as she came into the house along with laughing and looked like someone who was drinking at a bar or nightclub. She looked drunk. I didn't know who she was and didn't say anything as the house was filling up with company. I didn't know her then, her name was Bea, short for Beatrice Nocelli.

As years went on she seemed to be a little phony to me. She married Eddie and was a beautiful bride and had a beautiful wedding at a catering place called Arthur's at Bustleton and Byberry Aves. in Philadelphia, PA, that once was a furniture store called Furniture Village. Bea was half Italian and half Lithuanian but usually said that she was Italian. I don't know why. Later in years, when my daughter got married, Bea's daughter Francis was a flower girl in Nicole's wedding. When the time came to pick out gowns and head attire for the girls, Bea came along.

I found a Mary's bridal salon on Frankford Ave in the phonebook and we all met there. Nicole and I, together as mother and daughter, looked at gowns. She found a beautiful style gown by Larry Levine and similar to my bridesmaids and the flower girl in my wedding in 1970. Mary, the owner of the Bridal Salon, said she would make them from the same gown. When it came time to choose the headpiece there was a beautiful matching headpiece with a veil to cover your face as in a Roman Catholic Church when you get married and you only get married once in the Roman Catholic religion. The female bridal party had their faces covered with the veil just like the bride. Then you lifted your veil off after you walked down the aisle, at the altar. Bea, out of place at Mary's Bridal Salon, made a suggestion to my daughter of a velvet clip on bow for the female bridal party to wear at the back of their heads. I really didn't like the way it would look for a Roman Catholic Church wedding. I had seen the matching headpiece with the veil and tried to tell Nicole that this matches the gown, as I was giving her a formal wedding. There was so much disruption because of Bea, but Nicole and the bridesmaids wanted the hair bows and chose that style.

Mary, the owner, made them all by herself. I was not too happy of how it would look, but kept quiet, as it was my daughter's wedding. I chose my light, ice-blue suit gown with a matching hat and loved it, as I picked it from a formal bridal magazine and wanted that entire style from the clothes, to the hairstyle, to the shoe. I chose it all by myself of how I would look that day and night from the bridal magazine. When the day of the wedding came, Nicole looked beautiful but the bridesmaids looked terrible and one was pregnant and really showed her stomach. But it turned out okay and was a beautiful day and then later, an evening reception of my choice, which was a true Roman Catholic wedding.

The reception was at Fisher's Tudor House in Bensalem, PA, as suggested from a friend that Nicky grew up with as a teenager. She and I experienced a lot of good times after I married Nicky and I got to know her. Her name was Irene, and she married my husband's friend, Henry. Irene and Henry met as teenagers, but later divorced after they had two sons together. It was not love at all with these people who met and divorced. My husband told me about his friends that married and divorced so soon. It was a shame. I'm glad that didn't happen to me. Nicky and I and our families raised our daughter together. I, as time went by, did not like divorced people, especially the divorced people who were remarrying again to each other; to me, they were putting on a facade, and just wanted a big show that wasn't true in the eyes of religion, and making a mockery. Why even get married? It is too sacred and holy, and you are only lying to yourself.

There are people who want to be Catholic but never will be. I never went to church, as I had a lot of chores and maybe was just too tired, but I always was religious and christened a Roman Catholic. I say my prayers to myself, when I want or need to, for peace of mind. I love the beauty of the Roman Catholic Church as well as my communion, my wedding at St. Henry's church, as well as trying to steer our daughter toward that faith. This is what I was taught and that is what I love. People who aren't Roman Catholic always thought that we were rich. We were only rich in things. Before my husband died I told him, always believe in Christ, as he really was disbelieving, and in the end, he did.

The neighborhood, my father-in-law felt, was getting bad as years went on and it was. It was the people and their children who destroyed it for themselves, as well as everyone else. There were no morals or respect, and it was awful what I had experienced and seen in these people.

So we moved again. Nicky and I moved seven times in our married life, and it got too much for the both of us. The last house we bought was in Wissinoming, next to Tacony, in Philadelphia, PA, close to my twin sister girlfriends that I grew up with. We were only there for twenty-four years, and we moved again. It was beautiful, but as time went on, and in the first year, leaking pipes under the sink and destroyed everything. The original owner, whose name was Joel Rice, was a scam artist, trying to sell something he did not build, or have any know how. He kept trying to be friends with us and was becoming a pest. He said that he was going to move to Arizona, for which he did but kept coming here to Philadelphia PA, and to our house.

The house was a mess, with leaks from the kitchen. He was paid in full for the sale of the house, and there was no reason for him to come back. We had purchased the failing house, and my husband told him to stop calling. The next door neighbors also had a flood, and the mildew odor was getting stronger. There was a lot wrong and that house did not last. That is why Joel

Rice wanted to sell that house, because no one else was buying it. It was just a fancy looking house with steps that were not cemented, no railings on one entrance, no finished electric outlets, and an unmovable spigot that you could not move back and forth in the kitchen to put a standard large pot in. We stayed there for only five years and left. It was a very poorly built home and only looked beautiful.

It is a shame that happened. Nicky had a beautiful powder room installed downstairs with his guidance, but the leaks kept coming from underneath the kitchen sink and ruined all of the beautiful carpeting at the basement level where it was considered a den. Only really professional contractors and builders would have the know-how, skill, and strength to correct it, and I did not know this was going to happen in such a short period of time. But it was my last dream house before Nicky died some years later. He loved it, and I was close to my twin sister girlfriends, Erica and Joyce. We had a little Maltese dog as a gift from our daughter, and I named him from two previous owners, from Pee Wee to Caesar.

There was the famous Quaker City Flea Market on State Rd., in Wissinoming close to my girlfriend Joyce and her husband Johnny. I would take Caesar, the dog, every Saturday and Sunday to the Flea Market. At first, it was something to do. There was not a lot of good old things to buy at the flea market, but unexpected rain would come and ruin everything you may have wanted to buy. The flea marketers who sold items worked very, very hard, starting early at 4 AM in the dark morning hours, to be ready for people to come at 6 AM.

As time went on, I found beautiful things to decorate our house with from the flea market. I had decorating ideas in my mind and stuck to my ideas. We had our beautiful ivory French Provincial TV that was no longer working after having worked for twenty-five years, but it was a beautiful piece of furniture that matched the formal ivory couch and chair and we held onto it. I cleaned it with Murphy's Oil soap as I smoked cigarettes. Between all the cooking we did with frying and the use of the oven and my smoking cigarettes, it was turning brown. I was putting too much Pledge polish, trying to clean it and the TV cabinet was turning browner.

After discovering Murphy's Oil soap at a store and TV commercial from back in the 1980s, I took two weeks cleaning the plastic and wooden cabinet.

It turned out beautiful, but it was hard to do. It was such a beautiful piece of furniture with the enclosed TV and we just saved it and kept it in the parlor.

I loved mirrors. From the time we lived on 8th street in Hunting Park and Bustleton in Philadelphia, I was always decorating with mirrors. For me and Nicky's last house I found geometric mirrors that were a medium colored oak brown. I bought them at the Quaker City Flea Market and brought them home. I had leftover pure white flat paint and painted the wooden frames and the inside wicker bamboo with the white paint, around the mirrors. You were able to place the mirrored pictures horizontally or vertically. I purchased nails that would not damage walls that were thin and skinny if you wanted to take the pictures off, you could not see the holes. I experimented with the mirror pictures, placing them horizontally or vertically, and finally hung them in a vertical position and they looked diamond shaped, and the parlor looked bigger and modern. Nicky loved the way it looked and highlighted the French Provincial furniture along with the movie star mirrored pictures that he had bought so long ago in the 1970s in downtown Philadelphia, where he worked for W.R. Johnston, a printing company, of Mr. W.R. Johnston.

Every Saturday and Sunday at the flea market I would see things like this and if I could not carry something home with our dog, I'd bring Caesar back home as he tired and then go back to the flea market. It was a beautiful time. Nicky was seeing all the beautiful things I found and fun I was having. He was staying home watching the ball games and one day I said, "When a ball game was over, why don't you come to the flea market with me some Saturday or Sunday?" He had no desire to ever want to go to the flea market, but one weekend I told him, when there was no ballgame on TV, that they have hot dogs, water ice, bathrooms indoors, and a lot of people go there for the day. He went with me and Caesar that one weekend and then practically went every weekend thereafter. He found things that he needed and bought, whether the things were old, which that was the original idea of a flea market, and the flea market also sold new and not so new things, as time went on.

I decorated my last dream house, and I had a tropical kitchen, a New York styled parlor, an ocean-blue styled serene bedroom, and a little night club downstairs. I always would have loved a vacation home in Atlantic City, New Jersey, but Nicky and I could not do it, and the diabetes Nicky had, as time went on, was creeping up slowly even more and getting worse. He was insulin dependent, injecting himself five times a day and eating uncontrollably. He couldn't keep his weight down. But he was doing okay and managed it himself and was strong willed. I tried to keep him happy with this horrible disease. He made a lot of male friends through sports that he loved, and Nicky influenced them as he had a great personality and good sense of humor.

Prior to the diabetes, when we first met, Nicky's parents told me that he had been in a hit and run accident six years before we had met, but he never told me this, his mom did. So it was a double mishap of related health problems from the initial hit and run car accident to the adult diabetes when Nicky reached the age of forty, and it took a toll on me and our marriage. He was getting madder and madder and violent. I had to call the police for what was going on, as he was putting a strain on me and others. There was no rationality with him as time went by. The disease, as well as age, was taking a toll. And it was something I had to cope with. I kept busy with things that gave me happiness as well as our little dog.

I knew I would never love any man ever again. I had seen the rottenness in his sports friends and did not like them. I hated the football games he liked to get me to like or any of the other sports he watched and I repeatedly told him to find people to enjoy this with. I did not like these types of people at all.

I became, at our last house together, enjoying all the music we had. We had so much music that I didn't know all that we accumulated. I had music from when I was eight-years-old that I took care of and bought through the years as a teenager and that we had bought together.

We weren't having any parties, and I enjoyed it by myself. It was the perfect house to have big parties, but everything was getting ruined from the constant floods of the kitchen sink and we had friends that were acting childish and destructive in our home. Nicky did not want them at our home anymore. They were really fair weather friends as the saying goes, and very sloppy as time went on. It was time to put an end to inviting people to our house. And Nicky's family was the same. I did not want them with their surprise visits or to welcome them. They were foul-mouthed and argumentative and became unenjoyable and putting on a facade, as usual. As far as I was concerned, they were culprits to themselves, as well as Nicky and me, putting on a fake movie with their constant bragging, and with nothing to brag about or even to be proud of. They also were, an another old saying goes, Indian givers–when they give you something and expect something in return–and I did not want to be any part of their schemes. I had done a lot for them and they didn't even know it.

My in-laws and straight down the line of Nicky's family all expected something in return. The time finally came when it all ended in nothing but sorrow for them. There was too much disloyalty. There were too many second marriages that caused only problems. One thing I can remember, my true friends Erica and Joyce, were loyal. We never wanted or had any desire for each other's boyfriends, let alone husbands, who belonged only to them. That only made enemies. I never would fall in love or ever marry again, and I didn't want anything to do with Nicky's family. Neither did Nicky. Today most of them are dead and gone or divorced. If I would see any of them today, I would ignore them. They were a bunch of actors and actresses that you see in movies. And their party was over.

I had a lot of different types of jobs, even though I never graduated high school and I never will or would want to. Any job I did, I knew I did well. I worked for the famous J.C. Penney company first; I was a go-go dancer and dancer in the 1960s; I was a cashier for B.J.'s Wholesale Club; I was a salesgirl for the Dress Barn stores; I was a promotional model and salesgirl for major perfume companies; I was an Avon lady that promoted and had an interest in skincare, and sold and delivered like an old fashioned Avon Lady since 1982, without ever having a car like the Avon ladies of today. And in my childhood, I delivered the Inquirer Newspaper in my neighborhood of Port Richmond, with my twin sister girlfriends, for thirty-five cents a day. We also delivered mail for a mailman named Joe, for thirty-five cents a day. We sold lemonade for ten cents a glass with plastic cups all in the 1950s, before the 1960s came.

But my favorite career was dancing. Today in my senior adult years, I cannot dance like I did before, because of aging, but I would hope for young people who have the talent to make a career of it. And enjoy it while it lasts. And enjoy all of the dance TV shows of the past, as well as the movies about dancing. You might never be a famous known dancer like Fred Astaire or Ginger Rogers, but you can try to be and have fun along the way and you might even fall in love. I was only a follower of the granddaddies and grandmoms of dancing, by trying to follow their classic style and to keep a tradition of tap dancing like Fred Astaire or Ginger Rogers.

My daughter graduated from St. Henry's Roman Catholic school, where Nicky and I were married at the church and lived in the same vicinity. All of Nicole's girlfriends were graduating too, from St. Henry's Elementary school, to go to high school. They were all going to Ryan Catholic high school. Nicole was still taking tap dancing and ballet lessons at Anastasia's Dance Studio and was doing yearly dance recitals. Nicole did not want to go to Ryan Catholic High like her girlfriends. She loved tap dancing and ballet at that time and wanted to go to a school where she had school subjects such as English, Math, History, etc., in addition to being able to continue dancing. Nicole chose on her own to want to go to the High School of Performing Arts, here in Philadelphia PA. I was surprised that she had chosen this and happy that she would have the opportunity to advance in a possible dance career, but I told her not to get starry eyed, which means you can count more than your ten fingers of dancers that became famous like Fred Astaire or Ginger Rogers. But she was happy to be accepted at the High School of Performing Arts.

Nicole danced and studied her normal subjects and did very well. She was in the same school at the same time of the singing group Boyz II Men, who later became famous. Nicole was to go to high school for four years and graduated as a major in dance, as the school had originally said. She attended there for three years when a principal or dean said to her, and other girls, that she cannot be a dance major or just major in dance alone. She had to be a performing arts major and take other classes, such as drama, music, etc. Well, it was just too late to go into the last year there to take other classes and excel in the last year. It was unfair that they were not told this initially upon entering the high school. It disillusioned my daughter from this change. It also disillusioned other girls, and they quit and left the high school to go to George Washington High in the Bustleton area of Philadelphia. Nicole was not happy and neither were the other girls.

Upon going to George Washington high school for my daughter to graduate, they had said that now she could be a dance major and not have to take any other performing arts subjects such as drama, music, etc. It was too late, and the school board there made a terrible error. Nicole completed her last year to graduate from high school. She never took any more dance classes at Anastasia Dance Studio in Bustleton, as well as on Oxford Ave., I think that it was the Frankford section of Philadelphia. Nicole graduated high school with honors and then went to Jefferson University and became a doctor of occupational therapy. Nicole's real mother's name was Felicia, nickname Fay, after my mom. The Anastasia Dance Studio was just robbing parents constantly raising their prices, and they were not that advanced. The dance teacher and owner of the school was Grace Richards, and she had a dance studio partner named Sid. As time went on I thought, maybe Nicole would continue her dance education by being in plays or maybe even opening up her own dance studio, but that never happened because of the errors from Anastasia Dance Studio and the High School of Performing Arts in Philadelphia PA. It was not an interest to her anymore.

When I look back at my tap dancing teacher Karen, who never took a dime and was an excellent advanced teacher, who made me what I was as a dancer, and "you should have seen her dance and the way she dressed" and carried herself, "she really was a dance star," like my favorite dancer Fred Astaire, and Karen's favorite was Gene Kelly. We had gone through so much together, and it was something that I will never forget. She made me a big star but no one knew it. When I got married to Nicky, Karen used to say, "She'll be going down the aisle in roller skates," like when Barbra Streisand performed in the movie and my favorite musical, *Funny Girl*. I was married to a guy named Nick for forty-three years before he died, and the story is similar to that movie.

I never was conceited, and I never thought I was beautiful at all. It's a true old saying, "beauty is in the eye of the beholder," meaning the person who loves you and you love is really beautiful. And really, "beauty is only skin deep." It's very strange for me now that Nicky has died but I'm coping with it. Nicky was starting to get very strange old ways about him, for what, I or nobody knew. He became more bitter and bitter towards family and friends, as his health was deteriorating more and more from the diabetes. He became distant from people who cared and would say, "You don't care," like a child that can't have his or her way would. He knew there was no cure for his diabetes and this was his way of taking it out on those who cared for him. He had terrible moods most of the time, naturally because of the diabetes disease, and inflicted it upon others that were dear to him at one time.

I could remember before Nicky was so stricken with diabetes at the age of 40. He had no patience from his hit and run car accident at the age of 18. Most of the time he was argumentative in his conversations with others as his father was. His father also died from the diabetes disease. Nicky became distant and was having friendly unwelcoming relationships with people. He was not a happy man because of his two misfortunes in his life of the hit and run car accident, in addition to the diabetes that really affected his lifestyle, and most of all, his health. It was a great burden for me. I could not help him anymore, and he needed doctors and nurses care in a hospital type setting for the insulin that his body needed to live. All he kept saying was that he wanted to die.

He was able to come out of the nursing home when he felt well, as he wanted to be with me, but when he was with me, he would really not be happy because the disease of diabetes stood in the way. As strong as he may have been, he was weak at the same time. I brought him to places where there would be a level floor with no steps as he could not walk and used a motorized wheelchair. We went to restaurants, a shopping mall, Motown Theater shows that the disc jockey Phil Goldman hosted. He loved the casino to gamble, and we went to the Sugarhouse Casino in Philadelphia, PA. That is where my Uncle Frankie worked years ago, before it was a casino; before then it was where he made cane sugar, candy canes in boxes and the traditional Christmas green stockings made of plastic mesh and filled with candy canes that you still can buy in famous stores such as Walgreens, Rite Aid, CVS, etc. When contractors knocked down the old factory of the Sugar house, they decided to keep the old Philadelphia tradition and name of the Sugarhouse, where many hard working men worked and suffered like my Uncle Frankie. People today have the luxury of going to the casino, for not just gambling but the luxury of great atmospheres, dining, and music entertainment. I only wish my Uncle Frankie was here to enjoy the Sugarhouse casino. It was just his style. He was so high class after a hard day's work and always finely dressed and loved big supper clubs, as my grandfather Charles Embris built the Big Lit in Port Richmond where I grew up, located at Salmon St and Allegheny Ave., or Tilton St. and Allegheny Ave. where you really could see the old beauty of it.

I miss all the good times we had there. All my friends and family have died except for a few. So I won't be planning anymore big parties or weddings again. But I love the good memories of the past and try to capture them to stay happy within myself. I met some people, still keep in touch with some old friends, and dance when I can. I only wish I could tap dance again, but I cannot do the hard steps, as I have a condition in my ankles called tendinitis, permanently, from fractured ankles.

I contacted people to bring back the 70s disco music that was so lost, so the next generation could enjoy this music as well as dance or disco dance or even learn it. Radio stations must have agreed as it was such a huge success from it not being heard for such a long period of time, when I experienced this music at Harlow's night club in Philadelphia. Also I contacted TV stations to bring a dance show like I had on TV, to encourage the younger generation and that is how "Dancing with the Stars" came on and initially didn't start out great to catch onto viewers but look at it today from the early 2000s to 2015. It exploded and had to be a good idea when Lady Gaga, as time went on, made a debut on "Dancing with the Stars." History repeated itself from what I had. It gives anyone who loves to dance a lift of spirit. Then other variety shows followed, such as "The Voice," "The Idol," and "So You Think You Can Dance?" They are all great entertainment even if they're not great dancers.

You start at the bottom and work your way up and you can't do this forever as you do unfortunately grow older. But it's nice to hand it down like an heirloom to the younger generation as my tap dancing teacher Karen did. I also brought back modern-ness to Avon as it was getting stale with their tiny traditional jewelry. And I pushed for the sixteen inch necklace size to come to Avon, along with red lipstick. I brought back the color "Powder silver" to cars like we had in the 1960s by contacting a major car dealership, and I never even drove a car. I just love a more beautiful looking world.

Well some of my ideas must have paid off, as you can clearly see with your own eyes. What did I get personally from my ideas? The happiness of seeing them happy. Believe me, I did not get paid for these ideas. And I don't want to be on stage to receive an honor. And I'm not full of myself. Other people took my credit and that is okay. Because if I didn't enjoy doing this and putting my heart and soul into it, I would not have done it. I love turning back the hands of time of what I had and enjoyed, to give to the next generations as my ancestors gave to me. I like to see life as a happy musical, so the world is not gloomy. The everyday rut is boring and tiring, and this is a goal I've always had. When I go into a nightclub today and do some dancing, people cannot believe what they see and they come to me. We have fun and it's painful afterwards unfortunately, because I'm older. Dancing takes a toll on you and I had a lot of broken bones in addition to the pain of dancing as you age.

After our daughter Nicole got a little older, at thirteen-years-old, the printing industry was faced with a new way of printing–with computers and the computer world. The unions, of how the old printers were paid so well, like my husband Nicky, were not as strong anymore. The unions in the printing industry would make sure the printers were paid a good salary for the times and would negotiate with the printing companies. Nicky did not know about computers. It was a whole big change. He was tired and beat from all the hard work. He was laid off from work. It just got too much for him standing all day and working with a camera as he worked his way up, before we were married, going to his union school and becoming a photo compositor, also known as a "film stripper" that strips film. He printed material, like what you see in pharmacies, such as Flintstone's vitamins, box cartons, calendars, magazines. It was hard, standing all day, and you had to have perfect vision, and it was a lot of pressure to get the printing done quickly as companies need a printing job finished by a certain time. It was too much pressure from these companies.

So now that computers were doing the job, the companies didn't need as many printers. The real big companies like my husband worked for, such as Crown, Cork & Seal, that Nicky printed soda cans on metal and beer cans, were always large major companies and still are today. Nicky was proud to be a printer, following in his dad's footsteps. But it was getting too hard for him. One day he came home when we lived in Bustleton, a section in Philadelphia, PA. He had Ace bandages around his knees and could not walk very well. It was sometime in the early 1980s. I just looked at him and said to myself, "This man cannot do this anymore." It was taking a big toll on him physically. He had been working in extreme hot conditions, because the ink would freeze if there was any kind of air conditioning inside the factory. It was extremely hot in summertime, with temperatures outside of ninety-five to 100 degrees, in addition to the hot boiling ovens of the ink inside the factory. Maintenance was told to paint the floors that were originally natural, unpainted cement. Maintenance was told and given a shiny paint and painted the floors and in time the floor dried. But it now became even more dangerous as the floors were extremely slippery for anyone who even went inside the factory.

One day Nicky came home and his inside arm had been hurt as I could see. It was all stitched up and it upset me. Nicky told me how the floor was painted and slippery. He had slipped and fallen on large sheets of metal that were on loading trucks, and his arm was sliced really badly. He told me the story after he got home and it was horrible. When he slipped and got cut from the metal sheets, there was no one around at that time who drove a car, to take him to the hospital. He was bleeding to death from the metal tin sheets that he fell onto from the too slippery factory floor. Nicky got a towel from one of the workers quickly, wrapped it around his upper arm, which was his muscle, and drove himself to the emergency room, where he was taken care of.

Later he drove himself home and told me the story. That was one of another misgiving again, where he could have died from the stupidity of painting a factory floor with any kind of paint, let alone shiny paint, and he could have died. Time passed and since the computer business was taking over it was now their turn to suffer the consequences, as the big printing companies did not need or want the printers that were originally in the printing business. They wanted the "college men of computers."

Nicky left the printing industry and started working for the Housing Authority, with a big cut in pay from what he had been earning from the printing unions. It was hard for us, still raising our daughter, but we made it through. She was still a young girl, about eleven-years-old, and we were a family and happy. He would come home and tell me the fun times working for the Housing Authority and other men that Nicky made good friends with. He told me a lot of really true funny stories that made me laugh. He also got a good job in addition to the Housing Authority, both represented by the city of Philadelphia. We were okay and happy, and it was easier on Nicky. The change did him good.

Nicole was happy, she made a lot of new friends at George Washington High School, and in the neighborhood was close to her friends. I planned pajama parties where her friends and her cousins would stay overnight. We somehow always managed, because Nicky and I stayed together through thick and thin. He loved me and I loved him and we were typical young parents, struggling through married life, as well as life. A new game called "Atari," which to me was like a small pinball machine now that I think about it, was making its introduction and being advertised on TV commercials. Nicole was maybe around eight-years-old then. She was very close to her dad and I guess told him she wanted the Atari. Nicky got it for her, for Christmas, from "Santa Claus." She opened a lot of presents that Christmas morning and was really so happy and surprised when she got the new Atari game. But Nicky could not buy her the tapes at the same time to go with the Atari to actually play the game. After the holidays and New Year's, Nicky called up the company who made the Atari and told the company he'd bought one for our daughter but had no money left for tapes to play the games. Nicky was then laid off from the Housing Authority and explained this to the company. He had a lot of good traits about him, especially when it came to Christmas. After speaking to the company who made the Atari, Nicole got about four or five tapes to be able to play the game.

There's an old, true saying that goes, "It's better late than never," and another saying, "Good comes to those who wait." Nicole was so happy and her dad hooked up the game to our beautiful ivory French Provincial television set and started playing the Atari. It was a great game and as time went on she was a little wiz at it. It was something new to me and she wanted me to play, but I really didn't know how to play this game. She taught me. It was hard as you operated it with an electric paddle stick. I remember the tapes Nicole got and one was "Pac Man." Another was "Asteroids." And there were two more. We had fun as a family and Nicky played it and his parents came over and his dad played a game with his granddaughter. We were not at all good at this game like Nicole was, but it was really fun. It made for a merry Christmas that year.

The holidays were over and I took the large, white Sears department store artificial tree I had bought from the catalogue down. I put it up every year, along with other Christmas decorations, by myself. I loved decorating for Christmas and did it every year, when I was married to Nicky. As time went on, it was harder and harder. I cleaned everything before I put the decorations away and they lasted for years. I had decorations from when I was a little girl that I had bought for only ten cents. I loved the white artificial tree from Sears and Roebucks catalogue. I had red and white candy-striped small unbreakable satin balls from when I was a little girl and bought white and gold ones from Woolworth's and Kresge's five-and-ten cent store that I saved. I didn't have a whole lot of Christmas decoration but I had more than enough when it was time to take the decorations down, as relatives and friends always bought me something to add to our home.

It was getting too much for Nicky and me. His father did not help him at all and his father was in the printing business and didn't do anything when Nicky injured his arm. Nicky took it upon himself to bring major printing companies down. And Nicky won. He was a strong young man from all he had gone through, and we stayed together.

As time went by, I told Nicky I found a job in the newspaper and I would help out as he was laid off from the Housing Authority. Nicky was disillusioned as to what he went through with the printing industry and the Housing Authority in Philadelphia. He said, "You won't be able to find a job, no one's going to hire you," and I said, "I'll try." So I did, and found a job working for the Dress Barn. I started at the bottom and loved it. We were a happy family and I worked for B. J.'s Wholesale Club too. Then I found a job working for major department stores for the huge perfume companies. I loved all my jobs, and my career.

One of Nicky's cousins on his dad's side, named Nicole, found a job working with me coincidentally at the same Dress Barn in Philadelphia, PA. Nicole later married Nicky's first cousin Johnny's son, but they later, sadly, got divorced. They had no children. He was my favorite of all Johnny and Trixie's children. His name was William, and William grew up with our daughter. Nicole divorced her first husband, Barry, two years after getting married, but had no children together. Barry still really loved Nicole, but Nicole wanted a divorce as Barry wasn't committed or fit to be a good husband. He was too young in his way of thinking, and it was best they divorced. But it was a beautiful Roman Catholic wedding, and Nicole was a beautiful bride. I was happy that she had her dad walk her down the aisle. And Nicole was too.

I paid for the wedding, and Nicole helped with her money gifts for the bills we had later. It was a very expensive wedding with a lot of hard work. It cost Nicky and me the real reason to have a wedding and was worth every cent, along with all the planning and work put into it. My brother-in-law did not want us to have this wedding, and neither did my mother-in-law. It really came down to jealousy, and they had too much to say and it was not their place to. They were arguing constantly within themselves. Why even come to a wedding? Why? Is it because she was her grandmother and Donnie was her uncle? And she just wanted to make herself look good, or did she really want to just go to a big elaborate wedding? My mother-in-law did the same thing when it wasn't her place to for my wedding and then she and Donnie, after my father-in-law died, were doing the same thing for our daughter's wedding. They were just inappropriate. All they did was ruin everything in the end for themselves. They were sneaking, trying to sell the house my in-laws had lived in on Frankford Ave. close to Nazareth Academy, a Catholic school and college. It was after my father-in-law died that the rest of them were scheming and my husband caught them.

His family and a lot of his friends were trying to get me to go against him by inviting me to their parties without him long before our daughter was even married. But I was married to Nicky and we did or talked things over together. As time went on I seen how they all were sneaking around. Nicky would always say, and it was the truth, "they want what you have!" It was a real sin. Today, in the year 2015, I lost all of the luxurious things and beautiful homes and apartments we lived in and I'm happy thinking of all the good memories. I'm not the only one in the world who has lost homes or things that they loved, and I do without and keep to myself. The world to me now is full of too many young schemers who think they know it all and you can't trust them. They try and act like big business men and they aren't, they are just scam artists who talk too much, and they really cannot fulfill anything. I'll always believe in my ancestors, and how hard it was for them–especially how I seen them suffer, as my husband Nicky did, in the printing industry.

Before Nicky got sicker from the diabetes, I wanted to have my own supper club nightclub, and he told me how hard it was and you couldn't trust anyone. I could remember how hard it was for my boss Bill, who worked to build a decent night club. And I realized and took my husband's advice. I had a friend I thought would be a good business partner that kept secrets for five years from me, then she died. She told me right before I found out she died that she was an alcoholic. Nicky was right with the advice he had given me. I was thinking of a decent, high class nightclub or supper club, and I would never have been able to do this. It takes hard working men and knowhow and I never would have been able to do it. And if I did, I would probably end up just a lonely business woman.

Nicole got invited to her grade school reunion at St. Henry's Catholic School. I remember her telling me that there was a boy in St. Henry's with the same last name as hers, but there was no relation and I didn't think anything of it. It was just mere coincidence, although it was not a common last name. After Nicole divorced her husband Barry, she went to her grade school reunion. She had a good time with her grade school classmates and told me she was going to date the boy with the coincidental same last name. Nicole told him that she was married and divorced from her first husband. His name was Arthur. They started to date and I felt more content, as she was not a child or teenager that I had to look over anymore. She had her friends, she was driving and doing well. She stayed close to her cousin, Kimberly, and they were like sisters, for which I was content. So Nicole dated Arthur, and I really did not ask or get nosy, as she was an adult now. I didn't even see or meet him then. They dated for about a year and half and then she told Nicky and me that they were going to get married. Nicky and I were doing okay. They had gotten an apartment before they got married, like Nicky and I did, so they would have a place after they got married.

Nicole did a lot of traveling from high school and when she went to college at Jefferson University, here in Philadelphia, PA. She and Arthur wanted to get married in Jamaica. They planned their own wedding to be married there. Arthur's mother wanted to come but they wanted a private ceremony, just the two of them, and told her they were going to have another reception here in Philadelphia when they came back. They planned a reception in a place close to the airport called Albert's Cafe, in Northeast Philadelphia. I had met Arthur's mother, and we got along well. His mom's name was Donna, and she was a professional hairdresser with her own business. As time went on, Donna, Nicole's girlfriends, and I planned a wedding shower together. Donna was happy her son was settling down and getting married. Donna also had two other sons, but was divorced. She wanted to have the wedding shower at her home.

So we planned it, and I made meatballs with red gravy. The wedding shower was nice and Nicole's girlfriend, Samantha, who she grew up with, brought a cake made from the Acme supermarket with a tropical theme. I made little tropical plants with clay pots and glued jewels on them for favors to give the wedding shower guests. Nicole and Arthur then got married. I invited some friends to their reception at Albert's Cafe. Some of Nicky's aunts and uncles were still alive and they came. A lot of them were older now in their senior years. There was a disc jockey who was playing lousy rap music for the first three hours, and finally I went up to him and asked, "Do you have any

70s disco music?" And he turned it on, and my friends and some of Nicole and Arthur's friends danced to it the last hour of their wedding reception and had a wonderful time.

After they had their wedding pictures from Jamaica developed they gave Nicky and me some of them. I bought a small picture album to fit the size of the pictures. I bought white satin material with cotton batting and tropical seashells at Michael's craft store and made the cover for our parents' album. It was a beautiful Jamaican wedding they had, from the pictures I've seen.

As time went on our daughter was pregnant. Nicky, Janice and I were overcome with joy. As time went by, with the new ultrasound machines being used in hospitals, we could learn whether they were having a boy or a girl. Nicole had gone for the ultrasound and told Nicky and me about it; we were so happy we were going to be grandparents for the first time. But as time went on, Nicole gave us a surprise and said she was going to have twins. I could not sleep for a month worrying, as Nicole was a smaller sized woman. But the time came when she delivered the twins. She had a girl and a boy. They were six-and-one-half pounds each. They named them, Audrey, for the girl, and Richard, for the boy.

Nicole later divorced Arthur as he was not making a good husband or father. Arthur's parents, who were divorced, did not really help the situation. Nicole and Arthur invited Arthur's dad to the reception of Albert's Cafe. It was the first time I had seen him. He looked like a hippy with a ponytail in his hair and had a girlfriend that looked like a hippy with ugly tattoos all over her arms. Donna and her ex-husband did not set a good example at all, for the formality of the reception. Now it was two marriages that Nicole went through where the parents were divorced, and to me, they should not have even been invited to the wedding reception. Divorce was a bad reflection for a wedding, for a young couple. I remember that I would not let my mother come to my daughter's wedding with her first marriage to Barry for this reason. But it was not for me to say, as it was their wedding, and I kept quiet.

So Nicole divorced a second husband and raised the twins by herself. Arthur has no right to see the twins, now up to the year 2015. Nicole doesn't want anything to do with him anymore. The twins were born in the millennium year, as they called it, in the year 2000, in August. Nicole was doing fine and listened to her dad's advice, as Arthur was not doing the right thing as a husband or father. And so it was a second failed marriage.

Then Nicole met another young man, close to her age. She was happy working as an occupational therapist and raising the twins. She was on her own with being busy as a mother. We kept in contact with her after her divorce from Arthur, but we really didn't see or hear from her much. We spoke on the telephone occasionally and mostly she talked to her dad, as she needed her father's help now. I could not help her anymore. It was too much of a burden to me, keeping up with a house that had constant problems, taking care of our little dog and taking care of Nicky.

As time went by, Nicole brought home a guy she was dating, who she later married. I told her not to have any more children. She was forty-years-old now, and she had the twins. I felt she was too old to have another baby. Sure you feel good now and think you want to have another child, but your body takes a toll on you as time goes on and it gets harder and harder. She got married to this guy, and they had a child together anyway. She made it through, but now she and her new third husband will be facing an even harder time as they are not as young as Nicky and I were. They will never be able to get married in a Catholic church. Her new husband's name is Felix Borbello, and he adopted the twins.

The twins are now fourteen-years-old. I had never seen their little girl, but they brought her to visit Nicky when I put him in a nursing home. Nicky was slowly dying, and I knew that time was coming near. I phoned my daughter many times and told her that her father wanted to see his grandchildren, but she was too busy with her new married life for the third time. I called her when I knew he was failing more and more, and kept phone contacts with his doctor who visited him at Elkins Crest Nursing Home in Elkins Park, PA. I called our daughter when Nicky and I went to the Sugarhouse Casino, and he was transferred by his doctor to another nursing home. The last time I saw my husband Nicky was June 23, 2014, when we met to go there. Thereafter, I called our daughter and said, "I think this is it, he's not going to make it." I kept in contact with Nicole and the nurses and doctors by telephone. Shortly after that, when I called Nicole next, she told me he had died.

I don't see or talk with our daughter anymore, and it's best that way, as she has a lot of bitterness. As she once said to me, "I have my own life." Well, now I have my own life too. I've done the best I could for her, as a mother, and so did Nicky, as her dad.

Nicky is gone now, and it's hard to believe. We were married for so long, forty-three years. You never think you're going to get old when you're young. You just go about life and take it for granted. I spend my time now reading books, going to theater shows when there's a show that I'll enjoy, going to nightclubs and enjoying the music, and going to nice restaurants. I try not to take life for granted. It's strange to me sometimes, because now in my new life of being a widow, now that that Nicky died, I don't do what I did before as a wife and mother.

I do everything alone again, the way I did before I married. It's better that way. I could never have a relationship with anyone ever again. There's too much quarreling and too many arguments. The burden has finally left, and I'm free. I'm happy going out to nightclubs and just dancing by myself or with someone with no lasting relationship.

I'll die dancing!

# Acknowledgments

Maria Flaccavento, my editor, for her knowledge and professionalism; Misty Sparks, one of my idols; Sister Kathleen Sonnie, my right of way; my grandfather and grandmother, Stephen and Anne Putekis; my mother, Fay Putekis; my uncle Benny, Uncle John and Aunt Theresa; my tap dancing teacher, Mary; my best friends and twin sister girlfriends, Bonnie and Barbara; all of my friends from my childhood and adult years; school teachers, principals, and advisors; Philadelphia PA, the greatest and first city of the U.S.; Atlantic City, NJ, my favorite vacation for the summer; police officer, police commissioner, and mayor of Philadelphia, Frank Rizzo, and other police and official officers of Philadelphia; my dads that are a mystery; my husband, Nicky, and his family on both sides; our daughter Antoinette and all of the happy memories, and her children, our grandchildren; my three son-in-laws–Matthew, Christian, Anthony–and for only success and happiness to always be with them and their families and friends; all dancers, dance teachers and people that love the music and dances I love from the 1920s to today, and to the composers of the music, past and present, for keeping this great past with radio, TV and movies to inspire and make people happy; my favorite and first cousin, Joan Urquiza, and her husband Ben; neighbors we were close to as a family with morals; veterans who knew my uncle Benny, uncle John, and grandparents, who we stayed close to like a family with morals; Dr. Moffesses, Dr. Thresher, Dr. Mirabella and their families; the printers of famous corporations; the shoemakers; my favorite doctor, Dr. Puszinski, and his family, who when I was a child gave me my vaccination for diseases.